MAN UP!
RISE TO THE CHALLENGE

9 Truths to Encourage, Equip and Empower Every Man to Live Out His Destiny

Bernard K. Haynes

Man Up! Rise to the Challenge; 9 *Truths to Encourage, Equip and Empower Every Man to Live Out His Destiny*
by Bernard K. Haynes
Copyright © 2018 Lead to Impact™, LLC

For more materials and information contact:

Bernard K. Haynes
Lead to Impact, LLC
bhaynes@leadtoimpact.com
www.leadtoimpact.com

ISBN # 978-0-9961945-3-2
For Worldwide Distribution
Printed in the U.S.A

Edited by: Shannon Rasmussen

Published by:
Lead to Impact LLC
3740 Falls Tr.
Winston, GA 30187

Table of Contents

Introduction

"Commit your way to the Lord, Trust also in Him, and He will do it." Psalms 37:5

Man Up! Rise to the Challenge; *9 Truths to Encourage, Equip and Empower Every Man to Live Out His Destiny* was revised with more in-depth Biblical insight, powerful inspiration and practical instruction that can help men develop and implement a vision plan that will take their lives and families to a new dimension.

Each truth is a chapter based upon a Biblical man who overcame obstacles or challenges to live out his vision. Each message contains introspective and thought-provoking questions for men to answer to help guide them in formulating a vision plan for their lives.

If you are a man who wants to live at maximum capacity, or if you are a wife, mother, son, daughter, sister, aunt, friend or co-worker of a man that you want to see live at maximum capacity, then **Man Up! Rise to the Challenge** is the perfect gift.

I am not promising a magical formula or a guarantee that if you read this material, your vision will automatically happen. Nor am I promising that if you follow these truths, you will avoid obstacles or opposition. Just know that to walk in your vision, you must make sacrifices, overcome challenges, face opposition and work your plan. If you apply the practical information found within this interactive guide, you will be empowered to move in the direction that God destined for you.

In each of the nine truths, you will find yourself desiring things you never wanted, knowing things about yourself you never knew, and overcoming obstacles you never imagined. I pray that these nine truths open your mind and heart to everything God destined you to be and do. Not only will your life be affected, but everyone connected to you will be affected in a positive way.

Get Ready. Get Set. Man Up! Rise to the Challenge And Live Out Your Destiny.

Truth 1
Where Are You?

Part 1

Genesis 1-3

MAN UP!
RISE TO THE CHALLENGE

Where Are You – Part 1

"Then the LORD God called to the man, and said to him, 'Where are you?'" Genesis 3:9

Men get into serious trouble when they do not have a clear definition of who they are. In our fast-paced, technologically savvy, consumer-driven, twenty-first century world, men have confused their cultural, social and traditional roles with who they truly are. Men have allowed consumer marketing and branding strategies from corporations across the world to influence what they spend their money on, where they spend their time and who they become.

> *"Though no one can go back and make a brand new start, anyone can start from now and make a brand new ending."*
> *Carl Bard*

You will never be satisfied living a life that was not designed for you. God created you to be an original piece in His overall vision. You are unique. You are God's masterpiece. You were customized with a vision that only you can carry out.

There are more than seven billion people in the world. Of those seven billion people, none have your fingerprints and none have the material you were designed with. You are not a carbon copy of anyone. You are an original. When God created you, He destroyed the mold so that there would never be another man in the world like you. He created you to fulfill your purpose.

You cannot afford to waste valuable time and energy trying to be like any other man. God wants you to be you! If you are not you, then who is going to be you? Who is going to make the contributions to the world that only you can make? You were designed to live your purpose. Not your mama's purpose. Not your daddy's purpose. Not your friend's purpose. Not your pastor's purpose. Not the media's or someone else's purpose.

Where are you?

1. The Creation

"Then God said, 'Let Us make man in Our image, according to Our likeness; and let them rule over the fish of the sea and over the birds of the sky and over the cattle and over all the earth, and over every creeping thing that creeps on the earth.'" Genesis 1:26

When God created the earth, He didn't seek advice from the angels or call a special committee to take a vote. He simply spoke, and His Words came to life. His words were so powerful, so undeniable, and so irrefutable that everything came into being immediately.

In five days God created a spectacular world with His spoken word. He said, "Let there be light," and there was light. God spoke and dry land appeared that He called Earth. When He spoke, the oceans and seas were established. When He spoke, the sun, moons, stars and planets went to their locations to create our vast universe. The first twenty-six verses of chapter one in Genesis describe this incredible universe God spoke into existence. But on the sixth day, God created His greatest accomplishment: man.

> *"To be yourself in a world that is constantly trying to make you something else is the greatest accomplishment."*
> *Ralph Waldo Emerson*

There are two distinct keys in the above verse that need to be brought to every man's attention. First, God made man in His image. An understanding of who we are as men begins with knowing that we are made in His image. We were not created from some cosmic boom or evolved from an animal. We are the creative work of the God of the Universe. Man is different from every other created being because he was designed to reflect God's image.

God's design for man introduces a tremendous gap between human life and animal life. Though we may be similar biologically to certain animals, we are distinct because God created man to possess personality (knowledge, feelings and a will), morality (moral judgments and a conscience) and spirituality (communion with God).

What does it mean to you that God made you in His image?

Since you were created in God's image, how will this affect the way you live your life?

The second key to this verse is that God created man to rule over His creation. He gave every man the responsibility to rule. This does not mean that God no longer has authority, but that He gave man the responsibility to rule the realm of influence He entrusted him with.

God did not design man to rule as a dictator or dominator over others. Man is to rule under the authority of Christ. This kind of rule is a liberating leadership that equips and empowers not only the man, but everyone connected to his leadership. If you are not ruling your realm of influence God's way, then you are out of order.

What does it mean for you to rule under Christ's authority? If you have not been ruling under Christ's authority, what do you need to do to get in proper alignment?

Why is this kind of leadership liberating for you and those connected to you?

"Then the LORD God formed man of dust from the ground, and breathed into his nostrils the breath of life; and man became a living being." Genesis 2:7

When God created man, He made him out of the most basic element: the dust of the land. He did not use gold, silver, granite or gemstones to make man. He used dust, a miniscule particle that has no significant worth. Think about it. God used the small fine particles that you see flying in the air to create man to rule His creation. God not only formed man from the dust of the earth, He then breathed the breath of life into him. This is what separates mankind from all other creatures.

God could have chosen to create man any way He desired. He created man by using both natural material (dust) and supernatural power (His breath) to give man a unique place in His creation. The recipe of dust of the earth plus God's breath of life emphasizes the supernatural power of God and man's complete dependence upon Him. So your worth as a man does not come from society, who others say you are, what position you hold or what possessions you have. Your worth comes from God.

> *"When one door closes, another opens; but we often look so long and so regretfully upon the closed door that we do not see the one which has opened for us."*
> *Alexander Graham Bell*

A lack of worth influences men to believe Satan's lies: he reminds men of past sins, tells them they are inadequate, and tells them they are not good enough or talented enough. If you ever struggle with your worth, always remember that the creator is your source. If you are ever bombarded with feelings of inadequacy or worthlessness, remind yourself of who God destined you to be in Genesis 1:26.

Why is your worth not based upon society's views, your position or your possessions?

Why do you believe God would use something as insignificant as dust to create man?

2. The Garden

"The LORD God planted a garden toward the east, in Eden; and there He placed the man whom He had formed." Genesis 2:8

"Then the LORD God took the man and put him into the Garden of Eden to cultivate it and keep it." Genesis 2:15

God gave Adam the ultimate plan for his life. He made for him a lovely place where he could live in true peace and prosperity. He placed him in this remarkable garden full of trees that produced fruit: fruit that was beautiful to see and delicious to eat. Everything that God gave him in this wonderful garden was for his enjoyment.

What domain has God given you responsibility for, to work and watch over?

God put Adam into the most spectacular paradise the world has ever seen, to work and watch over it. Work is something good for man and was part of Adam's assignment before the fall. Just like Adam, God created every man to work and watch over the domain He gave him. It is not the government's responsibility, or anyone else's responsibility, to take care of your domain. It is your responsibility.

> *"I believe ingratitude is the original sin. I believe if Adam and Eve had been grateful for the Garden of Eden they had, they would not have been so focused on the one tree they didn't have."*
> *Max Lucado*

You are to work your area of responsibility to make it productive. You are to develop its full potential. You are to nurture it and cultivate it so that it continually produces to provide for your family and future generations. Work exposes your potential. You cannot expose the vision God gave you unless demands are placed on it by work.

Not only was Adam responsible for working the garden, but he was also responsible to watch over it. He was to guard the garden and its occupants at all cost against any threat. God intentionally built men physically and spiritually to protect everything in his care and under his covering. It is man's responsibility, therefore, to maintain God's presence in protecting his domain whether he is at home, work, or any other place in society.

What are you doing to nurture and cultivate your area of influence?

What are you doing to watch over and protect your area of influence?

What struggles are you dealing with in working and watching over your area of influence? What help do you need?

*"The L*ORD *God commanded the man, saying, "From any tree of the garden you may eat freely; but from the tree of the knowledge of good and evil you shall not eat, for in the day that you eat from it you will surely die." Genesis 2: 16-17*

God put the tree of knowledge of good and evil in the Garden of Eden to give Adam a choice to obey or disobey Him. God showed Adam the whole vision plan for His garden and everything He had created. He then gave Adam a direct command with all the information he needed to carry out His vision. Adam was free to do anything in the garden he wanted, except eat from the tree of knowledge of good and evil.

> *"How blessed is the man who finds wisdom and the man who gains understanding." Proverbs 3:13*

There was nothing essentially evil or magical about the tree or the fruit on the tree. It is unlikely that the fruit had any intrinsic power that gave Adam any more knowledge than he already had. The presence of this tree was good because, for Adam to be a creature of "free will," there had to be a choice whether to obey or disobey God.

If God had not given Adam the choice, he would have essentially been a robot, simply doing what he was programmed to do. God created Adam with "free will" to choose between right and wrong, good and evil. In order for Adam to truly be free, he had to have a choice.

God desires our love and obedience to Him. He desires for us to choose to follow His directions. It hurts his heart when men choose to disobey His directions. He yearns for us to choose Him, but He will not force us to choose Him.

The lesson for men to learn today is that when God says no, it is for our own good. Disobeying Him and going our own way will always lead to disaster. God, our creator, knows what is best for us, and when He says no to something, we should listen and obey Him. When we choose to obey our own wills instead of His perfect will, we suffer the consequences for our disobedience.

What choice have you made recently that was contrary to God's direction for your life?

What was the consequence for making this choice? Were others affected by your choice?

What can you do to make better decisions?

3. The Helper

Then the LORD God said, "It is not good for the man to be alone; I will make him a helper suitable for him." Genesis 2:18

For the first time, God saw something that was not good: that man was alone. He wanted man to be in intimate relationship not only with Him, but also with someone to help advance His Kingdom. Adam was created for relationship, and it is impossible to have a relationship alone. With the creation of woman, Adam experienced a powerful relationship that would bring the joy of love for another person. God's "blueprint" for creating woman was to fulfill her purpose by being the man's help meet.

Everything in her draws her to help. God created woman to be man's ideal partner. The woman was not created above or below Adam but as a complementary partner to help Adam live out his God-designed vision.

Why do you think God said it is not good for man to be alone?

What does it mean for woman to be a suitable helper for man?

God gave Adam the vision plan and how to work it and Adam was to include his wife with all the details so they could work together to fulfill it. God gave man the responsibility and the accountability to be the vision leader in the home and gave to the woman the responsibility and the accountability to help him make the vision happen.

> *"Let the wife make the husband glad to come home, and let him make her sorry to see him leave."*
> *Martin Luther*

This verse can hit some men hard because they are guilty of trying to handle everything on their own thus leaving their wives out of the process. This was not God's intention. Not only did God design the woman to be a helper, but he also designed her as an equal partner in advancing God's Kingdom. She should be respected and honored as such.

How can you involve your wife or future wife in your life?

God's desire is for men and women to work together as a unit, complementing one another and not competing against one another. Building one another up and not tearing one another down. Loving one another until death do them part and not throwing in the towel when things get tough.

When a man is aligned with God's plan, he understands that his wife or future wife is not his enemy but his partner in helping him bring God's vision to fruition. He realizes she is not his maid or servant, but a part of him. Adam summed it up in Genesis 2:23 by saying, "…She shall be called woman, because she was taken out of man."

What will it take for you and your wife or future wife to become a formidable team?

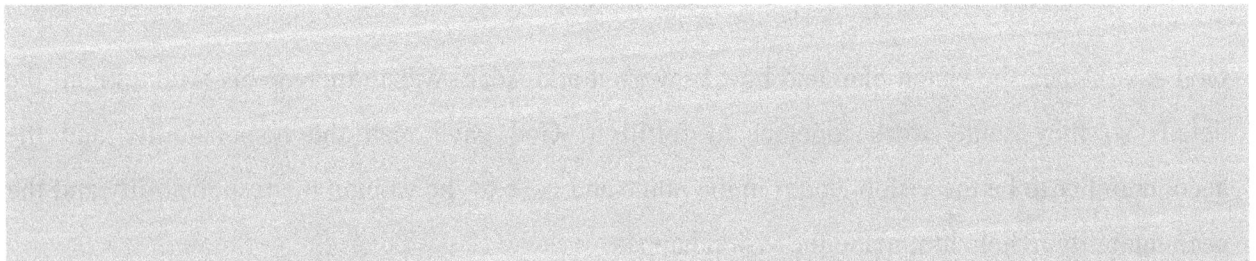

"When you stop chasing the wrong things you give the right things a chance to catch you."
Bernard Haynes

16

Truth 1

Where Are You?

Part 2

Genesis 1-3

Where Are You – Part 2

"Then the LORD God called to the man, and said to him, 'Where are you?'" Genesis 3:9

4. The Assignment

"¹⁹Out of the ground the LORD God formed every beast of the field and every bird of the sky, and brought them to the man to see what he would call them; and whatever the man called a living creature, that was its name. ²⁰ The man gave names to all the cattle, and to the birds of the sky, and to every beast of the field, but for Adam there was not found a helper suitable for him." Genesis 2:19-20

God did something truly amazing for men through Adam. When He created Adam, He brought His animals to Adam and gave him the right and authority to name His creation. He created Adam to be a visionary and leader. Stop and think about the profound implications of this great responsibility. God gave man naming rights over his creation. He gave man the right to speak blessings over that which came under his leadership.

What people or situations do you need to speak blessings over? Write out what you would say.

Pay close attention. The scripture says, "Whatever the man called a living creature that was its name." There was no discussion. No explanation. No second guessing. Whatever Adam named it that was its name. Giving something or someone a name in Biblical times was significant. They did not give a name with a unique spelling just to be different; they did not give a name because it was currently in style; and they did not give a name to impress their family and friends. They gave a name that had significance and stood for something. It signified purpose, expectation and makeup.

18

What is possibly more satisfying than knowing the God of the universe gave men the authority and responsibility to name things? For man to be in position to name something or give it its identifying purpose is significant. A name predetermines and establishes the expectations for what that person or thing is to become.

> *"The cost of not following your vision is spending the rest of your life wishing you had."*
> *Bernard Haynes*

But in order for a man to properly name someone or something, he must be under God's authority. If a man is not under God's authority, he will incorrectly name things. He will name things that don't belong to him. He will claim things that belong to other men. If a man is out of God's will, he will not only name things incorrectly but he will hinder his growth and progress. And because man is not an island to himself, others who are depending on him – like his wife, children, relatives, community, church and co-workers – will be negatively affected if he name things inaccurately.

Why is a name so important and what should it signify? What value do you put on a name?

What must you do to get under or stay under God's authority so that you correctly name the things under your authority?

Many men can't say who they are because they have no clue what their assignments are. Many men are floundering without a vision or pursuing a false vision that is based on contemporary society's values. And these values are usually contrary to God's values. God desires men to have a vision for their lives and families that comes from Him and belongs to them personally, and not a vision dictated by our culture, current trends, man-made religion or someone else's image of what their life should be.

> *"Do not pray for easy lives. Pray to be stronger men."*
> *John F. Kennedy*

Our world is in desperate need of men who speak life over their wives, empower their children for excellency, stand strong in their communities and inspire others to live their best lives. Don't let our twenty-first century fast-paced, instant gratification, every-man-for-himself world block you from walking in God's assignment for your life. God has provided you the necessary tools to live out your assignment effectively: the presence of His Holy Spirit, His Word, your spiritual and natural gifts, and a desire to succeed.

Many men need to get back to the place where they are living out God's original assignment so that they can hear the voice of God and follow His directions. God always provides the resources for the assignment He gives. The Garden was God's provision for Adam to carry out his ultimate assignment and where you are right now is God's provision for you to carry out His assignment for you and everyone connected to you.

How will you use the tools God gave you to live out His assignment for your life?

If you know your assignment, how can you live it out? If you don't know your assignment, how can you find it out?

5. The Fall

[4] *"The serpent said to the woman, 'You surely will not die!* [5] *For God knows that in the day you eat from it your eyes will be opened and you will be like God, knowing good and evil.'* [6] *When the woman saw that the tree was good for food, and that it was a delight to the eyes, and that the tree was desirable to make one wise, she took from its fruit and ate; and she gave also to her husband with her, and he ate." Genesis 3:4-6*

When most men read Genesis 3:6, they can't help but bring out the fact that Eve ate the fruit first. The truth of the matter is that Adam was responsible. God gave Adam a very specific vision for him to carry out. He was to work and watch over the land to develop its potential and guard it from any threat. He was to provide for all those under his care.

Adam allowed the enemy to strip him of his position. He was God's assigned representative to carry out His vision in the garden. Instead of Adam fulfilling his assignment as leader and

> *"God is responsible for the consequences of our obedience; we are responsible for the consequences of our disobedience."*
> *Charles Stanley*

visionary, he allowed the enemy to deceive the woman while he stood in silence.

Satan brought his temptation against the woman because he perceived she was more vulnerable to attack. Maybe Satan knew by observation that Adam didn't do an effective job in communicating to her the vision the Lord gave him. This failure on Adam's part made her more vulnerable to temptation.

Why would the serpent target the woman?

Have you fully communicated your vision to your wife or future wife?

The entire time the serpent was talking to the woman, Adam was present. Instead of Adam taking the lead and standing up to the serpent, he chose to remain silent. He gave his leadership responsibility to the woman, thus setting a contrary agenda against God's plan for the family.

Adam's silence caused him to relinquish his God-given right to lead to become a follower. Instead of accepting responsibility for his sin, he blamed the woman. Adam said, "The woman whom You gave to be with me, she gave me from the tree, and I ate." (Genesis 3: 12).

The disease of silence still distracts men today. Many men have allowed the women to enforce the discipline at home. Men have turned over their spiritual leadership to the women. Women have become the vocal leaders for leadership in many homes and churches. I realize there are exceptions, but too many men are on the Amber Alert: they are missing in action.

What things have you remained silent about instead of speaking up?

Why does silence continue to plague men in the 21ˢᵗ century? What steps can men take to break through the silence barrier?

Not only has the silence of men been a distraction, but men's inability to accept responsibility has been a major flaw. Instead of loving the fact that they are men created with the responsibility to lead by nature, when it was time for Adam to step up and accept responsibility for his sin, he blamed Eve. The man said, "The woman whom You gave to be with me, she gave me from the tree, and I ate." Genesis 3:12

Adam's attempt to blame Eve is completely consistent with human nature. Instead of owning up to their sins and bad decisions, too many men have a habit of blaming others for their circumstances. Instead of taking ownership, they shift the blame to someone else. Many men thrive on playing the blame game instead of accepting responsibility. They blame their spouses for lack of support, their parents for lack of love, their company for unfair treatment, the government for failing to help, the economy for being weak, and the list goes on and on.

It was Adam's choice to blame Eve and disregard his responsibility. It cost him dearly. If you desire to grow to your full potential, you must accept responsibility, take ownership, learn from your errors, make any necessary changes and lead forward. The choice is yours.

What are some ways men (including you) have tried to shift the blame to others?

What area(s) of life do you need to accept more of an active responsibility for? What actions do you need to take to be more responsible?

6. The Question

"They heard the sound of the LORD God walking in the garden in the cool of the day, and the man and his wife hid themselves from the presence of the LORD God among the trees of the garden. Then the LORD God called to the man, and said to him, 'Where are you?'" Genesis 3:8-9

God created man to rule the earth while He ruled the heavens. But man disobeyed a direct command from God and ate of the fruit from the tree of life and death. Adam's disobedience caused them to be cast out of the Garden of Eden. But before God cast the man out of the garden, he asked an important question that still rings true today: "Adam, where are you?" Genesis 3:9.

Instead of Adam confessing what he had done, he tried to hide from God. That was a big mistake. When faced with a question in your life about where you are, you can boldly tell God where you are and what you need. You do not have to hide or be afraid, because He is there to help you. You don't have to blame your job, your family, your spouse, the government, society or God.

If God asks you the question "Where are you?" what would you tell Him?

It is the trick of the enemy to make you think that running from God is the answer. The enemy is only out to steal, kill and destroy the destiny God designed for your life. He is after your self-esteem, your identity, your mind, your emotions, your plans, your witness and your productivity. He is after everything you value and hold dear.

One day, men will realize they cannot hide from God, and they will come clean of all their sins and allow Him to renew and restore them back to Him.

What sin(s) have weighed your life down that you need to confess before God? Romans 12:1
"…let us also lay aside every encumbrance and the sin which so easily entangles us, and let us run with endurance the race that is set before us."

When God asked Adam the question, "Where are you?", He definitely knew Adam's location. He knew he had deliberately disobeyed His command against eating the forbidden fruit. Adam's guilt and fear caused him to attempt to hide from God. All God wanted him to do was to be honest with Him and come clean about what he had done.

I believe it would have been a different outcome if Adam had sought God for forgiveness. God would have bestowed His restoring favor on him and Eve. God was waiting for Adam to tell Him where he was and what he had done. This was Adam's opportunity to reflect God's character. Instead, he ran and tried to hide from the all-knowing God.

What bad decisions have you made that cost you?

If you are outside of God's plan for your life, stop what you are doing and ask for His forgiveness so He can restore you and guide you back on the right path. Even if you blew it, God can put you back better than you were before. When He puts your life back on track, He begins by giving you a greater sense of who He is and what He has purposed you to do. You stop making excuses, blaming others and hiding in fear.

> *"Don't let the negative noise of yesterday drown out the sound of your vision for a better today and greater tomorrow."*
> *Bernard Haynes*

Disobedience broke their fellowship and hindered their relationship, just as it does with us. God loved Adam and Eve so much that He restored them. He loves us enough that, through Christ, a way has been made for us to renew and restore our relationship and fellowship with Him.

God is calling, "(**Your name**), where are you?" Stop making excuses. Stop procrastinating. Stop allowing yourself to be intimidated by those who say you cannot make it.

Listen to God! Take heed to His directions! He provides everything you need to execute His plan for your life. He has everything set up for you, but He is waiting on you. He is waiting for you to trust Him. He is waiting for your faith to connect with His purpose. He is waiting for you to tell Him where you are so He can put you on the road to your destiny.

What sin or sins do you need to ask God to forgive so you can get in position to lead the way He wants you to lead? Write them down here.

Now that you have asked God to forgive you of your hindering sins, what action steps can you implement to prevent these sins from burdening you so you can lead more effectively?

"Trust in the LORD with all your heart and do not lean on your own understanding.
In all your ways acknowledge Him and He will make your paths straight."
Proverbs 3: 5-6

Truth 2
Man UP! Rise to the Challenge

Part 1

I Samuel 17

Man UP! Rise to the Challenge

"Then it happened when the Philistine rose and came and drew near to meet David, that David ran quickly toward the battle line to meet the Philistine." I Samuel 17:48

What giants are you facing? Are you facing giants that make you feel incapable and inefficient?

Is living from paycheck to paycheck and barely making ends meet a giant in your life?

Is struggling in your marriage or training your children a giant in your life?

Is being unemployed or under-employed a giant in your life?

Is struggling with low self-esteem or a lack of confidence a giant in your life?

Our world is in desperate need of men who will stand against the giants that come up against them. Our families, communities and churches need men of character, consistency, courage and commitment whose lives inspire women, children, relatives, co-workers, and other men to do better, climb higher, achieve more and live better. We will take a look at David's story of victory over Goliath in the next two chapters, and the nine truths it exposes that will help you defeat your giants.

1. Pronouncement from your giant

"He stood and shouted to the ranks of Israel and said to them, 'Why do you come out to draw up in battle array? Am I not the Philistine and you servants of Saul? Choose a man for yourselves and let him come down to me.'" I Samuel 17:8

> **Man Up!**
> *Be strong and rise to the challenge with the courage to accept your responsibilities as a man, despite situations or circumstances that may make you want to quit and throw in the towel.*

Your giants will call you out. They will tell you what they will do to you and those connected to you. They want you to doubt what God said is possible for you in His Word. They want you to worry about your circumstances today and what the future holds for you tomorrow.

Goliath really did not have to say a word; his stature alone made men tremble in their shoes. He stood close to ten feet tall. He had a coat of mail that went from shoulder to knee and weighed between 175 and 200 pounds. And that was just his armor. He also wore a bronze helmet and leggings and he carried a bronze spear. And to top it off he had a "shield-carrier that went before him carrying a shield the size of a man." Goliath was intimidating. (I Samuel 17:4-7)

The giants in your life can seem like impassable roadblocks or insurmountable mountains that stand in the way of your progress. They will come at you with the intention of destroying everything you hold dear in your life: your health, your peace, your dreams, your vision, your marriage, your business, your children, your finances, your joy and your faith.

Every man faces giants at some point in his life and it does not matter how much money he makes, how many degrees he earned or what

> *"There are no secrets to success. It is the result of preparation, hard work, learning from failure." Colin Powell*

side of the tracks he is from. Giants do not discriminate. You may not want to face a giant but it is inevitable that you will. When your giants attack you, they will come with an arrogance of sure victory, and their discouraging words will leave you dismayed and afraid like Saul and the men of Israel.

"Again the Philistine said, 'I defy the ranks of Israel this day; give me a man that we may fight together.' When Saul and all Israel heard these words of the Philistine, they were dismayed and greatly afraid." I Samuel 17:10-11

Trying to avoid your giants won't make them stop harassing you. Hoping they will magically go away won't work. It is not that easy to face giants. As you will learn through this study, you must face your giants in order to defeat them.

What giant(s) are you dealing with right now in your life?

What are your giants telling you that you cannot do?

"The Philistine came forward morning and evening for forty days and took his stand." I Samuel 17:16

Goliath was the obstacle standing in the way of Israel's victory. He did not issue his challenge one time and leave. For forty agonizing days, every morning and every evening he called out Saul and the Army of Israel. For forty days Goliath flaunted his size and strength daring Saul to send a man to fight him.

I don't know what giants you are dealing with that are challenging your manhood. I do not know what the giants in your life are telling you. Your giants may say, "Why are you studying this

> *"When you can do the common things of life in an uncommon way, you will command the attention of the world."*
> *George Washington Carver*

material? You are only going to fail." They may ask, "Why are talking about living a better life with your messed-up background and past." They may remind you that, "You can't make positive change because the last time you tried you blew it."

Your giants want you to surrender before you even try. They want you to keep making excuses that hinder your future progress. They want you to believe that you will never live beyond your current circumstances. Your giants want you to focus on your past, squander your present and forfeit your future.

Men live with different pressures -- spiritual, physical, mental, relational or financial handicaps that can limit their effectiveness. These pressures can leave men going in circles, never living to their full potential. Listed below are key life areas that men struggle with. Discuss in detail what you need to do differently or how you can improve in each area to overcome the pressure from your giants and live your best life.

A. Relationship with God:

B. Relationship with your spouse, fiancée or other close females:

C. Relationship with your children:

D. Relationship with your family and friends:

E. Finances:

F. Physical health:

G. Work, Career or School:

H. Thought life:

I. Social life:

2. Perceive your situations differently

"What will be done for the man who kills this Philistine and takes away the reproach from Israel? For who is this uncircumcised Philistine, that he should taunt the armies of the living God?"
I Samuel 17:26

In my opinion, there's no greater story in the Bible than the story of David versus Goliath to teach men important spiritual insights about how to perceive situations differently. Perceptions vary from man to man. Different men perceive different things about the same situation. But more than that, men assign different meanings to what they perceive.

> *"The ultimate measure of a man is not where he stands in moments of comfort and convenience, but where he stands at times of challenge and controversy." Dr. Martin Luther King, Jr.*

Goliath was merely a mortal man defying an all-powerful God. David looked at the battle from God's point of view. If you look at giant problems and impossible situations from God's perspective, you will realize that God equipped you with everything you need to win your battle. But, if you look at your situation through your eyes or the eyes of other men, you will see the size of your situation as unconquerable.

Goliath wants you to stay stuck where you are so you won't attempt to challenge him. He wants to suck the life out of you with his fear tactics so you will live in constant mediocrity. He wants your perception of him to be one of fear and frustration like the men of Israel. When King Saul and the men of Israel heard the words of Goliath, they ran and hid like scared children.

"When Saul and all Israel heard these words of the Philistine, they were dismayed and greatly afraid." I Samuel 17:11

"When all the men of Israel saw the man, they fled from him and were greatly afraid. The men of Israel said, 'Have you seen this man who is coming up? Surely he is coming up to defy Israel.'"
I Samuel 17:24-25

As humans, we are subject to the perception problem that the men of Israel and Saul had about Goliath. We judge people on the basis of surface appearance. We focus at the externals and we form opinions that are out of line with reality.

Goliath had all the tangibles that would impress and intimidate the strongest of men. David, on the other hand, had been given the ability to see as God always sees, and he was neither impressed nor intimidated with the size and history of Goliath.

Why do you believe the enemy's attack against men is so intense?

What challenges are you dealing with right now that cause you to run and hide?

How can you gain victory over the challenges you listed? Who or what can you incorporate in your life to help you overcome your challenges?

When David heard the threats of Goliath against the Army of Israel, he was confused as to why the men of Israel were hiding in fear. David asked them, "Why are you running in fear?" and they responded by saying, "Have you seen this man who is coming up?" (I Samuel 17:25) He couldn't believe that the men of Israel allowed the uncircumcised Philistine to defy the armies of the living God.

> *"Anxiety in a man's heart weighs it down but a good word makes it glad."*
> *Proverbs 12:25*

The men of Israel perceived Goliath as an unbeatable force. Even King Saul, who was qualified to fight Goliath, hid in fear. The scriptures say that Saul stood head and shoulders above everybody and he was God's assigned leader of the people. (**Read I Samuel 9:1-2)** But Saul was a coward because he perceived that Goliath was bigger than God.

In contrast to King Saul and the men of Israel, David perceived the situation differently. He was not overwhelmed with the size and stature of Goliath. Neither was he impressed nor intimidated by the giant's threat. He knew no matter how big the giant was, his God was bigger. And no matter how powerful Goliath might be, his God was all-powerful. David's perception of God made Goliath look like a dwarf in his eyes.

How do you perceive your giants? How do you perceive your God?

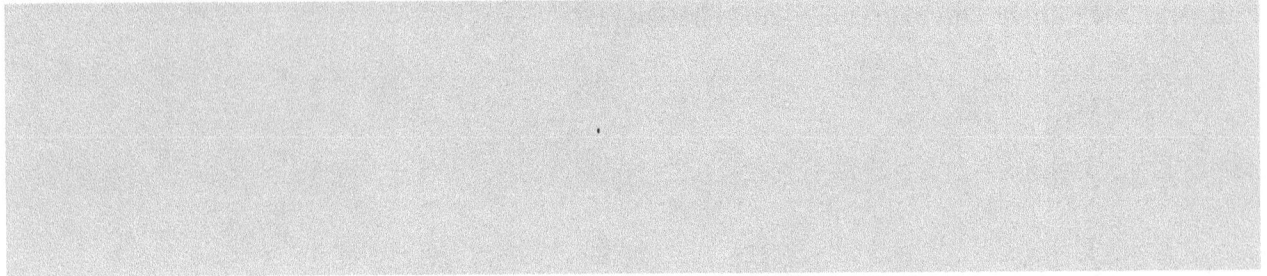

As a man of God, you must have the same unwavering perception as David; that no matter how big the giant or the magnitude of the obstacle, you can overcome through the power of God. You must believe that if God gives you a vision, He equips you with the tools and resources to accomplish it.

While you cannot control others' perceptions of God and the giants of life, you can choose to focus on the greatness of God. Refuse to allow negative perceptions to corrupt your mind and refuse to allow the inaccurate perceptions others may to have derail you.

> *"It always seems impossible until it's done." Nelson Mandela.*

Challenging a giant is not based on your age, stature, position or possessions. You do not need a background check or someone else's permission. David is your prime example; he was a young shepherd boy who was sent by his father to check on his brothers in the military. And while he was on this mission, he heard the taunts of Goliath against God's people. **(I Samuel 17:12-23)**

When you perceive your situations differently, you see victory when others see defeat. You see possibilities when others see impossibilities. You take action while others talk about what they are going to do. You walk by faith when others are paralyzed by fear.

How do you see yourself? How do you see the world around you?

Do you take action based upon what God has assigned you to do or is your behavior dependent upon how you feel others will view you? If you base your actions on how others will view you, what changes can you make to move in the direction God desires you to move?

3. Participate in your purpose

"Let no man's heart fail on account of him; your servant will go and fight with this Philistine."
I Samuel 17:32

Saul and the Army of Israel hid in fear for forty days waiting to hear someone say he would accept the challenge and fight Goliath. But to hear those words from the mouth of this young boy who had no background in military combat seemed like a cruel joke. The good news is that someone finally stepped up and wanted to fight Goliath, but the bad news was that he was a young shepherd boy.

> *Your response to God's purpose for your life is the single most transforming event, and all else flows from it.*

David's bold statement seemed ridiculous coming from a teenaged shepherd boy. He was not a champion warrior nor was he experienced in the latest military battle strategies. He did not make this statement haphazardly because of the heat of the moment, nor was he trying to impress Saul and the men of Israel. It may have seemed to others that this was just youthful pride and overconfidence, but it was not. David may have been a young shepherd boy, but he knew God and understood his purpose.

The question may be posed, "How did he know his purpose at such a young age?" The reason he knew his purpose was because he spent time talking and listening to God while he kept his father's sheep. He used his time of keeping sheep to learn about God, responsibility, and his life's purpose.

Where you currently are may not be the ideal place. You may be in a place of discontent, or discouragement, but God can reveal or reestablish your purpose. Do not think because of your current position or status that God cannot use your purpose to shine before the world.

How can you participate in your purpose?

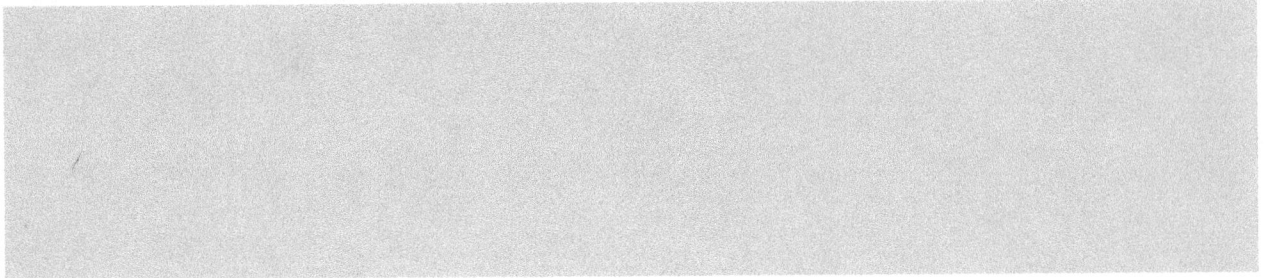

Goliath was nearly twice the size of David, but this did not faze David. He was confident in his ability to challenge the champion warrior. His inner motivation prevented him from accepting things the way they were.

David's motivation didn't come from the men of Israel, because they were too busy hiding in fear. His brothers didn't motivate him, because they were criticizing and finding fault in him. (I Samuel 17:28) Saul didn't motivate him, because he was too busy telling David that he was too young to go against the giant. (I Samuel 17:33)

David's inner motivation prevented him from letting Goliath disrespect God and His people. He knew that this situation couldn't go on for another day. He knew that he could not walk away and let Goliath win. Something had to be done. Someone had to step up to the plate and take on the challenge from this seemingly undefeatable giant.

What truly motivates you? The "why" should provide the motivation and the desire you need to

> *"More men fail through lack of purpose than lack of talent." Billy Sunday*

participate in your purpose. There are millions of men who have great intentions and many ideas but who never achieve anything of significance because they lack the motivation to participate in their purpose. Every man needs the kind of motivation that Randy Slechta speaks of:

"Motivation supplies you with the courage to look at yourself in the mirror and realize that you can achieve more than you have. It drives you to be better than you ever have before, propelling you to great heights of success."

Are you willing to participate in your purpose even when the odds are stacked against you? Or will you make excuses for why you cannot do it?

There are more than seven billion people in the world and God created every individual with an original purpose. God uniquely designed you so that even your fingerprints distinguish you from every other man on the planet. He did not make any carbon copies. He did not create you to participate in someone else's purpose. You were created to participate in your purpose.

The enemy of your purpose wants you to be an imitator. He knows if you waste time trying to be someone that you are not, you forfeit your purpose. When you do not live your purpose; you become a hindrance in your marriage, with your children, on your job, in your family, with your finances and living your vision.

Today is your day to participate in your purpose with confidence and courage. And when you do, you will accomplish things you only dreamed of accomplishing. Your innovative ideas, creative concepts, and tremendous thoughts will rise to the forefront and you will see your life grow beyond everyone's expectations.

Ask God to guide your thoughts as you meditate about the direction for your life. Answering these eight questions will help you realize your God-given purpose and will position you and others for success.

1. What are your unique God-given gifts and abilities? How could using these talents and gifts serve, help, and contribute to your family and community?

2. What are your deepest desires that scare you to death? How can you shake the fear and move forward?

3. What unique life experiences (positive or negative) forced you to trust God? How can these life experiences help you realize and live out your purpose?

4. What would you do with your life if you weren't worried about the difficulty, the time it takes, or the money you make?

5. What choices can you make to break free from a comfort zone and trust God with living out your purpose?

6. What can you do when God's purpose goes contrary to your desires? What role does faith play?

7. What do you want your eulogy to say? Write it out and live it.

8. What legacy do you want your purpose to leave for future generations?

Once your purpose becomes clearer, you need to create an overarching purpose statement. Your purpose statement is who you believe God created you to be. From your answers to the eight questions about purpose, write down your overarching purpose statement and begin to live it.

My Purpose Statement:

4. Proceed with authentic confidence

"And David said, 'The LORD who delivered me from the paw of the lion and from the paw of the bear, He will deliver me from the hand of this Philistine.'" I Samuel 17:37

David was confident that he could defeat Goliath despite the giant being nearly twice his size and a seasoned warrior. David's confidence did not resonate with Saul because he thought David was disqualified to challenge Goliath because of his age, size, and inexperience. Saul said:

"You are not able to go against this Philistine to fight with him; for you are but a youth while he has been a warrior from his youth." (I Samuel 17:33)

This expression of doubt from Saul showed that he looked at the battle purely on appearance. He

> *"Argue for your limitations and, sure enough, they're yours." Richard Bach*

counted David out because he did not look the part of a warrior. Saul essentially told David, "He's been a soldier longer than you have been alive. How can you ever defeat him?"

People will count you out before they know anything about you. They will quickly judge you by your appearance or where you come from and perceive in their mind what you are cable of doing or not doing. Before they even hear your story or know where your heart is, they will predetermine your status. The old cliché may ring true in your life as it did with David: "Don't judge a book by its cover."

Name a time when you were judged based upon appearance or what someone else said? How did it make you feel?

Give an example of a time you had to show confidence after being rejected. What was the outcome?

Man is impressed with the externals, but God looks at the heart. People judge individuals by what they wear, what they drive, what others say, or where they live. Don't let anyone tell you what is possible in your life based upon what they see externally. Let them know what they see on the outside is not who you are on the inside.

> **"Whether you think you can or think you can't, you are right." Henry Ford**

God was preparing David for his battle against Goliath while he was a lowly shepherd. I Samuel 17:34 says, *"But David said to Saul, 'Your servant was tending his father's sheep.'"* Shepherding was not a glamorous or high-echelon occupation. At the time of David, shepherding was left to the youngest in the family, or to slaves. David was a committed shepherd who took his job seriously. We learned from I Samuel 16:30 that after he was anointed to be the next king, instead of quitting his day job, he went back to tending his father's sheep.

God wants to see how you will conduct yourself while keeping sheep. He is watching your character when others cannot see you. He is paying attention to how you handle your current responsibilities. He is watching to see if you are faithful with a few things to see if He can trust you with more.

What three character traits do you value the most? Why do you value these traits?

When David challenged Goliath, he was prepared for battle. While David was shepherding, God was preparing him for the day he would accept Goliath's challenge. David probably did not know in the beginning that his menial job of keeping sheep would ultimately prepare him for his eventual confrontation and victory over Goliath. Please do not take it lightly when you are keeping sheep because God can use your experience with the sheep to equip and empower you for victory over a major challenge.

When a lion and a bear came and took a lamb from the flock, David killed both.

"I went out after him and attacked him, and rescued it from his mouth; and when he rose up against me, I seized him by his beard and struck him and killed him." I Samuel 17:35-36

This is generally God's preparation pattern for men. He calls a man to be faithful right where he is and then uses his faithfulness to accomplish greater things. If David had run in fear of the lion or the bear, he would never have been prepared to fight Goliath. God is waiting for men to trust Him so He can empower them to defeat the giants in their lives.

How can you remain faithful during your preparation time?

46

In the midst of our preparation, we rarely see how God will use us. But, we can look back with confidence and know that the same God who delivered us before will deliver us now. Your authentic confidence in God's ability to work in and through you positions you for success. It is not rooted in a self-built, self-conceived confidence, but it is centered on a complete trust in the purpose God gave you to offer to the world.

> *"The tragedy of life is often not in our failure, but rather in our complacency; not in our doing too much, but rather in our doing too little; not in our living above our ability, but rather in our living below our capacities."*
> *Benjamin E. Mays*

David knew if God had previously delivered him from the attacks of a lion and bear, He had the power to deliver him from Goliath. He walked in authentic confidence and relied on what God could do in and through him and not an arrogant self-confidence that relied on his own strength.

"Your servant has killed both the lion and the bear; and this uncircumcised Philistine will be like one of them, since he has taunted the armies of the living God." I Samuel 17:36

David knew that even though everyone was counting him out, God had counted him in. He was confident that Goliath would be defeated that day. Goliath stood as a threat to his people, his future kingdom and his promised kingship. His desire was rooted in seeing God's people free of an evil and oppressive enemy.

While everyone assumed David would easily be defeated, David knew victory was possible. He knew God was on his side and his deep confidence in his ability to rid the world of Goliath was his reason for going against the odds.

What threats prevent you from living with authentic confidence in who God created you to be?

What action steps can you implement to overcome the threats you listed above?

"If you really put a small value upon yourself, rest assured that the world will not raise your price." Author Unknown

48

Truth 2

Man UP! Rise to the Challenge

Part 2

I Samuel 17

Man UP! Rise to the Challenge – Part 2

"Then it happened when the Philistine rose and came and drew near to meet David, that David ran quickly toward the battle line to meet the Philistine." I Samuel 17:48

5. Perform in battle with your tools

"He took his stick in his hand and chose for himself five smooth stones from the brook, and put them in the shepherd's bag which he had, even in his pouch, and his sling was in his hand; and he approached the Philistine." I Samuel 17:40

Before David defeated Goliath with a sling and a rock, Saul tried to outfit him with his armor. (I Samuel 17: 38-39) Saul's armor didn't work for David because it did not properly *fit him*. Saul's armor was too big. Imagine watching this scene: a young shepherd boy putting on the armor of the king, who was much bigger than him.

This scene had to be hilarious because you have this boy that wears a size 30 putting on the size 52 extra-long armor of the king for battle. And to top it off, David tried to carry a sword that he could not even

> *"I don't fear the man who practiced 10,000 kicks one time. I fear the man who has practiced one kick 10,000 times." Bruce Lee*

hold up. David looked ridiculous and he knew it. He knew that he could not fight in Saul's amour because it did not fit. David finally told Saul, "I cannot walk with these, for I have not tested them. "

David refused to use Saul's armor to fight Goliath because it was unfamiliar to him. Instead, he used the tools that he was familiar with to fight the giant. In the eyes of those around him, his tools looked insufficient to challenge a champion giant.

Your tools may not look like tools built for champions, but if God gave them to you, He expects you to use them. Do not compare your tools to any other person. He gave you exactly what you need to win your battles. He can take what looks insignificant and use it for a significant victory. He can take what others say will not work and use it to do a great work.

Have you ever tried to use someone else's weapons to fight your battle? What was the outcome?

Often men make the mistake of trying to fight their battles with another man's armor. They see God do something awesome through someone else and they try to copy it. What works for one man may not necessarily work for you. Men fail repeatedly in their battles because they do not trust God with the armor He gave them.

I struggled for years with the attempts of trying to use another man's armor instead of trusting God with armor he equipped me with. I lost battle after battle because I was using unfamiliar tools. And trust me that is not the way to fight your battles. I had a major breakthrough in my life when I realized that I could be me and God would use me. I could fight with what He equipped me with and win despite what my tools looked like or what other people thought.

> *"Do not let what you cannot do interfere with what you can do."*
> *John Wooden*

So often when facing giants, men forget what they should remember and they remember what they should forget. Men remember their defeats and they forget their victories. Many men can recite the failures of their lives in vivid detail, but they are hard pressed to name the specific remarkable victories God has pulled off in their past.

It is easy to fall victim to this way of thinking because of the negative and pessimistic world that we live in. It is easy to succumb to our giants (greed, anger, lying, arrogance, sexual lusts, hatred, fear and worry) when we don't use the weapons God equipped you to use. It may look crazy going against the giants in your life with simple tools, but if God sends you then He can take care of you.

What weapons are at your disposal to use to fight your battles (see Ephesians 6: 10-20)?

How can you effectively use each weapon to win your battles?

6. Possess a progressive mindset

"This day the LORD will deliver you up into my hands and I will strike you down and remove your head from you. And I will give the dead bodies of the army of the Philistines this day to the birds of the sky and the wild beasts of the earth, that all the earth may know that there is a God in Israel."
I Samuel 17:46

David did not challenge Goliath with negative and fearful talk. He didn't say, "I can't," or "I don't know how I am going to defeat this giant." He didn't stammer, stutter, or second-guess his assignment. He challenged Goliath with a progressive mindset that victory was possible.

When you have a progressive mindset, you won't allow the giants in your life to stop your forward progress. You will think positively, speak with authority, and move in action even in the face of a crisis.

How can you have a positive mental attitude when you are faced with a negative situation?

Goliath thought David was a joke. He felt that sending David was an insult to his manhood. He said to David, *"Am I a dog that you come to me with sticks... Come to me and I will give your flesh to the birds of the sky and the beasts of the field."* (I Samuel 17:43-44) Goliath approached David with an arrogance of sure victory. He underestimated the heart of his opponent by judging his outward appearance.

Goliath wanted to intimidate David, but David would not be intimidated. David stood against Goliath boldly. He walked in the assurance that victory was possible. Most men won't admit it but they are intimidated by their giants. They talk big and bad in front of people but when they are alone they cry like babies.

> *"Death and life are in the power of the tongue and those who love it will eat its fruit." Proverbs 18:21*

The giants leave them hurt, confused and desperate. Because of the size of the giant, men can begin to focus on the odds against them. They forget they have a God that is bigger than their giant, who wants to use them to conquer their giants. I wonder what God must think, when all the while He has promised us victory. *"But thanks be to God, who gives us the victory through our Lord Jesus Christ."* 1 Corinthians 15:57.

What is possible in your life and family when you decide to stand against your giants?

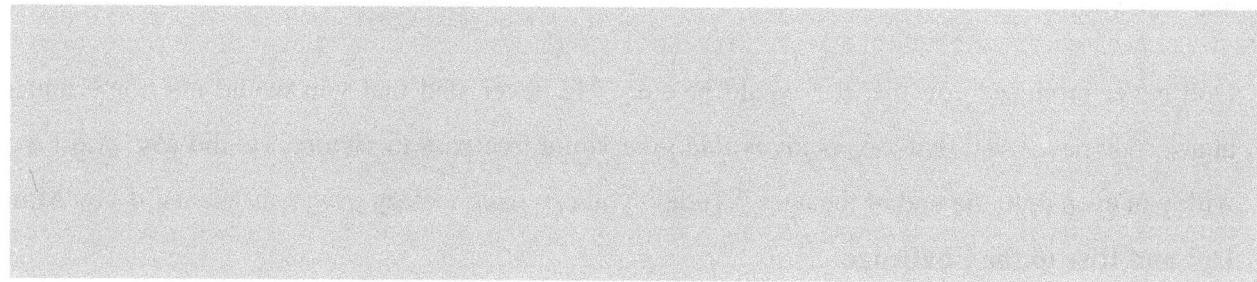

David stood against the giant with eyes fixated on God. Intimidation played no part in his life. With incredible confidence in his God, David told Goliath what was going to happen to him. David knew the battle belonged to the Lord.

You cannot go it alone, because Goliath is too big and strong. You may be a highly-skilled and talented man. You may have many years of practical work experience and more degrees than a thermometer. But in order to take out Goliath, you need someone on your side that is familiar with all of his tactics and tricks. You need someone with you that is bigger than your giants. You need someone you can trust no matter how sticky and ugly the situation may get. You need the God of the universe to lead and direct you.

I do not know what giants you are confronting that are challenging your manhood. I don't know what the giants in your life are telling you. Your giant may tell you that you lack the background and skill set to succeed. He may remind you that you failed the last time you tried.

Your giants want you to surrender before you even try. They want you to keep making excuses that hinder your future progress. They want you to believe that you will never make it to your promise. They want you to keep blaming others for where you are. Your giants want you to focus on your past, squander your present and forfeit your future.

You can live a successful life by following God's direction. Trust me. God sees and knows your giants, your fears, your goals, your temptations, your worries, and your dreams. He is there to help you succeed. If family or friends walk away, He will be there. If things get worse before they get better, He will never leave you. If you lose your possessions, position, or prestige, He will not abandon you.

God never promised you that life would be easy. He never said that you would not come under attack. He never said that the enemy would give you a free pass to victory. He did say, "Lo I am with you even until the end of the ages." Today, you can have victory over your giants, if you **Man Up! and Rise to the Challenge.**

What are two challenges in your thought life that you must overcome to live your best life?

What actions must you take to overcome the two challenges you named above?

7. Put your faith into action

"Then it happened when the Philistine rose and came and drew near to meet David, that David ran quickly toward the battle line to meet the Philistine." I Samuel 17:48

No one in the Philistine or Israelite camp had their money on David. Everyone, including Goliath, figured that this was going to be an easy victory, but David knew otherwise. He knew that in spite of Goliath's stature, God had equipped him to win the battle.

David put feet to his faith. Instead of running in the opposite direction from his obstacle, he ran toward it. He did not just talk a good game about how he was going to defeat Goliath. His faith showed through his actions.

It is time to shut your mouth and put your faith in action. It is time to stop talking about your dream and develop a plan and execute it. Victory comes when you take your eyes off your obstacles, fix them on God's vision and move in faith.

What area of life do you need to put feet to your faith and take action?

What are the action steps you will take?

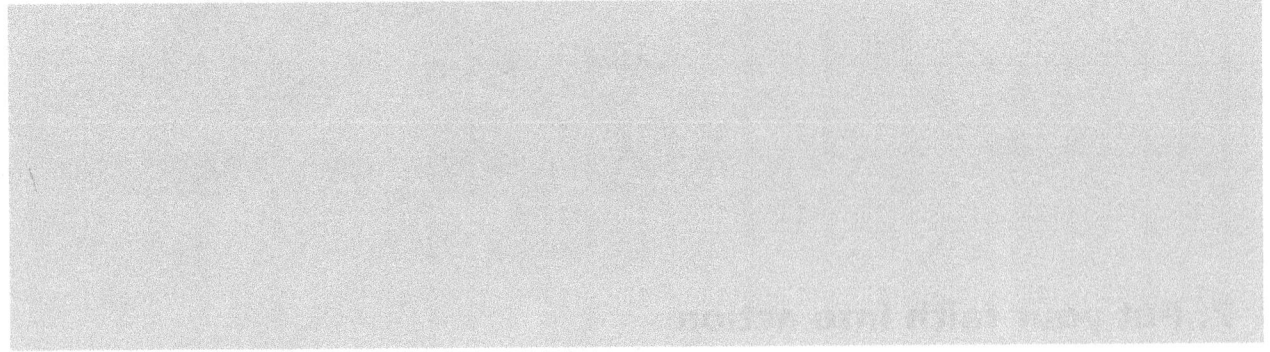

Many men struggle at this very point. Is God supposed to do it or am I supposed to do it? The answer is, "Yes!" God does it and we do it. Trust God, rely on Him, *and then get to work and work as hard as you can – run right at the enemy.* That is how the work of God is done.

David had a clear and concise goal, to take away the reproach against God and Israel. No enemy was worthy to stand and disrespect the God that David loved and served. David refused to let Goliath stand in the way of his ultimate assignment: to take him out. He knew without a shadow of a doubt that the giant was going to be defeated that day.

Visualize this picture: David, a young shepherd boy, approaching a man nearly twice his size. He was the kind of man that you wanted on your side in a back-alley brawl. From a human perspective, David had all the odds stacked against him. He was just a young shepherd boy that had no experience fighting giants.

> *"Every man and woman is born into the world to do something unique and something distinctive and if he or she does not do it, it will never be done."*
> *Benjamin E. Mays*

If you want to be in a different place than you currently are; you must develop an overwhelming inner motivation to change. You must focus more intensely on where you want to be and begin to make the necessary changes to get where you desire to be. You can't wait for the right person to push you to get there. You can't wait for the right season to get ready. You can't wait for something magical to happen to motivate you to move. You must motivate yourself to move.

You may ask, "How can I motivate myself to achieve greater things when I am discouraged by where I currently am?" I suggest that you seek God's face and read His word to see what He has to say about who you can become and what you can accomplish. If you spend more time focusing on what He has to say, your inner motivation to succeed -- which He has equipped you with -- will kick in and propel you toward your vision.

In what area of life do you need to put feet to your faith and take action?

8. Prevail over your challenges

"Thus David prevailed over the Philistine with a sling and a stone, and he struck the Philistine and killed him; but there was no sword in David's hand." I Samuel 17:50

David prevailed over Goliath because he exercised his faith in God. His assurance that God would give him victory was his defining moment. Everyone thought David did not stand a chance against the giant, but they failed to realize that he had someone bigger than Goliath on his side.

No matter how big your challenges seem, be assured that you can stand against until it falls down completely when you trust God to help you overcome it. God is much larger than any obstacle you'll ever face. So rather than look at the obstacle that's standing in your way right now, look at God, who stands ready to help you overcome your obstacles.

What challenge(s) stand in your way of living a better life?

What actions can you take today to prevail over the challenge(s) you named?

When you focus on how great God's power is, you'll be able to see your problem from the right perspective and gain the confidence to know that you can handle it with God's help. When David stepped to Goliath, he only had his bag with his sling and five smooth stones. He did not waver nor did he let Goliath's stature deter him. He reached into his bag, grabbed his sling and slung one stone that struck the giant on his forehead causing him to fall on the ground.

"And David put his hand into his bag and took from it a stone and slung it, and struck the Philistine on his forehead. And the stone sank into his forehead, so that he fell on his face to the ground." I Samuel 17:49

Notice he did not have to use all the stones. It took one stone that was aimed in the right direction. David was prepared for this moment. He had spent many days in the field practicing his marksmanship with the sling and rock

> *"We can complain because rose bushes have thorns, or rejoice because thorn bushes have roses."*
> *Abraham Lincoln*

and defending the sheep from their predators. His tools did not look like much but they were weapons of destruction in hands of a skilled marksman.

What unconventional skills or talents has God given you to fight your giants?

How can you use these skills or talents to their maximum capacity?

God, your Creator, knows every detail about what you're dealing with; He cares deeply about it, wants to help you, and is capable of helping you win. You must choose to see your obstacle as an opportunity to cultivate your character and increase your faith while you trust God to lead you through the process of overcoming it.

God's plan for your life may seem unconventional from your limited human perspective. But whenever you decide to trust God's plan, you can count on God to keep His promise to never leave you through your toughest challenges. The more you focus on God's power, protection, and provision, the less fear you'll feel. As God reveals his plan to prevail over your challenges, simply follow it the best you can day by day. Be willing to say "yes" to whatever God asks you to do even when it doesn't make sense to you or others; you will make real progress to overcoming your challenges.

> *"Even if you're on the right track, you'll get run over if you just sit there" Will Rogers*

Every day, choose to take whatever next steps God leads you to take. Don't give up when you're frustrated that your obstacles seem to be too much to handle. Instead, remind yourself that God is in control and pray for the strength you need to be patient and persevere. Ask God to help you avoid the distractions and discouragements that will come from internal and external voices. And ask Him to give you true accountability partners to encourage you to keep pressing forward whenever you feel like quitting.

You can prevail over your giants when you walk according to God's purpose for you. It may not be easy, but God never said life would be easy. He did say "I will be with you always even until the end of the world." Because of this assurance, just like David, you can prevail over your challenges.

James 1: 2-4 states, "My brethren, count it all joy when you fall into various trials, knowing that the testing of your faith produces patience. But let patience have its perfect work, that you may be perfect and complete, lacking nothing." Your trials will test your faith. James says that our trials teach us patience and equip us to live a meaningful and fulfilling life. How has a particular challenge you have experienced made your life more meaningful and fulfilling? How did this trial test your faith? Describe your thoughts in detail.

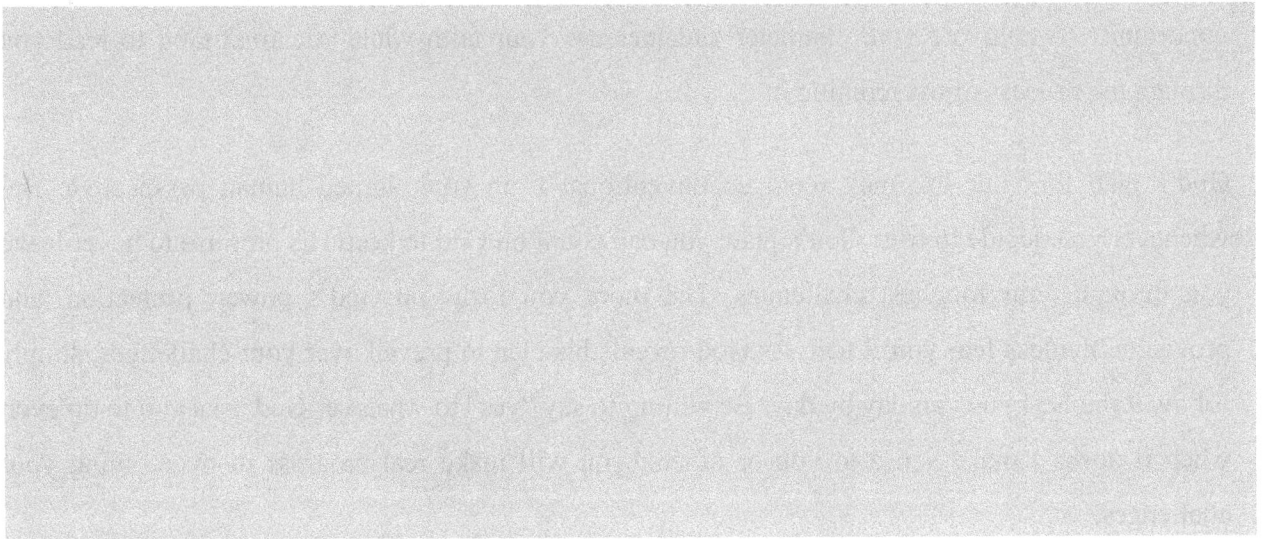

9. Position others for success

"The men of Israel and Judah arose and shouted and pursued the Philistines as far as the valley, and to the gates of Ekron. And the slain Philistines lay along the way to Shaaraim, even to Gath and Ekron." I Samuel 17:52

You were created with an original purpose in mind to make an impact in the world. The only way to make the impact God designed you to make is through the eyes of faith. The fact that you are alive right now, that you have endured through extreme pressure, and that obstacles could not take you out is evidence that you have a purpose that will allow you to positively impact others.

David was counted out by his father and family because of his position. The men of Israel and King Saul thought there was no way that a lowly shepherd could defeat a

seemingly indestructible giant. But God counted him in because of his heart's attitude. He was in the perfect position for God to use him to gain victory over Goliath and empower the men of Israel to defeat the Philistine army.

God can use you where you are to prepare you for a greater blessing. It may not look like it or feel like it, but never think because you are not in the position you desire or because you are doing what others think is menial work that God cannot advance you.

David's victory over Goliath was not just for him to receive notoriety and accolades. His goal of defeating the giant was for the entire nation of Israel. His success over the seemingly undefeatable giant positioned an entire race of people for victory.

What motivates you to succeed and help others to succeed?

David ran toward a giant who was a champion warrior twice his size with only a sling and five rocks because he understood the power of faith in God. He knew from past experiences that God could be trusted. He understood that living by faith was bigger than him; it was about obeying God's direction and delivering a nation from the ruthless Philistines.

When you walk by faith and are striving and growing to reach your maximum potential, you are on your way to lasting success. But there's one more important part to the success journey: helping others. Without that aspect, the journey can be a lonely and shallow experience.

> *"And do not neglect doing good and sharing, for with such sacrifices God is pleased."*
> *Hebrews 13:16*

Our most lasting and fulfilling achievements are often earned by helping others fulfill theirs. Helping others is something you can do right here, right now, whether it's spending more time with your family, developing an employee who shows potential, helping people in the community, or simply putting your own desires on hold for the sake of your family. The key is to link your vision, values, purpose and goals with your desire to help others.

Victory over your obstacles is more about others than you. There are people connected to you who are waiting for you to overcome your obstacles. They will never utter a word to you, but they are watching and listening from a distance. Your victory will give them the confidence that if you can overcome your obstacles, then victory is possible for them.

How can living out your purpose help position others (your wife, children, co-workers, mother, father, siblings or friends) succeed? Name at least three people you can help position to succeed.

What are the best ways you can help the people you named above succeed?

"Everybody can be great … because anybody can serve. You don't have to have a college degree to serve. You don't have to make your subject and verb agree to serve. You only need a heart full of grace. A soul generated by love." Martin Luther King, Jr.

Truth 3

Realize Your Vision

Habakkuk 1-3

MAN UP!
RISE TO THE CHALLENGE

Realize Your Vision

*"Then the L*ORD *answered me and said, 'Write the vision.'" Habakkuk 2:2*

Do you have a clearly written vision that will impact your life, family, community and the world? Visions are birthed in the heart and mind of a man who is frustrated and tired of the way things are in contrast to the way he believe things could and should be.

It was the vision of equal rights for all people that inspired Dr. Martin Luther King, Jr. to crusade for civil rights. It was the vision of a new nation of people that led Abraham to leave his homeland to follow God to an unfamiliar land. It was the vision of greater discovery that motivated George Washington Carver to discover over 300 different uses for the peanut. It was the vision of becoming a fisher of men that led Peter to leave his fishing business to follow Jesus. Vision demands change.

What is Vision?

Vision is a crystal clear mental picture of a preferable future that God communicates to a man. The man becomes so committed to the vision that he will pursue it despite any obstacles or challenges.

What is possibly more satisfying than knowing the God of the universe designed you with a unique vision to impact the world? His vision for you is not a one-size-fits-all, but it is uniquely fashioned to fit you. No matter who you are, what country or continent you live on or what side of the tracks you are from, God created you with a specific vision that no one in this world can live but you.

There are men who have great positions at work, who earn excellent incomes and drive nice cars, who live in big houses in gated communities, but who are frustrated and tired with life. There are men who go to church, participate in ministry, read the Bible and give tithes and offerings, but who feel their lives are out of sync. There are men who spend their days standing on street corners, in and out of jail, playing childish games and living unproductive lives because they do not know God has a greater vision for every area of their lives.

When a man realizes the power of his customized vision designed by God, he will change his approach to life. He will understand that it is his responsibility to look out for his future and the future of those connected to him. He will not allow the distractions and disappointments of life to keep him locked in the status quo or drowning in mediocrity. He will take the initiative to develop a vision plan and go to work.

Why does vision matter?

Now is the time to unlock the power of your vision. This section is derived from my book and workbook Vision Impact. After spending quality time studying and meditating on Habakkuk 2:1-4, I extrapolated seven keys to help men unlock the power of their vision. If you implement these seven keys, your vision will have a powerful impact on your family, friends, community, city, country and world.

1. Vision is revealed when you are in position to listen

"I will stand upon my watch, and set me upon the tower and will watch to see what he will say unto me and what I shall answer when I am reproved. Then the Lord answered me and said, record the vision…" Habakkuk 2:1-2

For you to unlock the power of your vision from God, you must first reside in your personal watchtower to listen for His directions. In ancient times, watchtowers were built on city walls so watchmen could see their enemies or messengers approaching their city from a distance. From the watchtower, they could see the enemy approaching and alert the people in enough time to prepare for battle.

The prophets used the picture of the watchman and watchtower to emphasize an attitude of expectation. Habakkuk went to his personal watchtower expecting to hear from God. He knew this was the place and time to listen to how God would answer his perplexing questions.

> *"A kingdom man moves according to what God's instructed him to do, thus ruling his world rather than allowing everything and everyone else to rule him."*
> *Tony Evans, "Kingdom Man"*

Do you have a personal watchtower from which you can hear from God? Wherever your watchtower may be, a room in the basement, the living room after everyone is asleep, an early morning walk or a quiet place in the park, you must get alone with God.

You need to make sure your time alone with Him is uninterrupted. When you go to your watchtower, you need to put away your mobile devices, turn off the television, close your Facebook page and tell your family and friends not to disturb you unless it is a serious emergency.

Your daily time in your personal watchtower is your time to meet with God and hear His directions. You will need a Bible to read and study what He says. I recommend the New King James Version or the New American Standard Bible.

You will need a pen and paper. Take a journal or your Man UP! Workbook to record what He speaks into your life. The last thing you will need to bring is an open and receptive ear to listen to His guidance.

You do not have to come with any games or gimmicks. You do not have to worry about the right words to say or a special prayer formula. You do not have to line up all your ducks in a row or possess all the correct answers. You can come to Him in an honest, humble and specific way to let Him know what is on your heart and mind. When you share your heart's deepest desires, the God of the universe will respond with His directions for your life and/or family.

What do you need to do to get in position to hear God's direction?

What things or people do you need to eliminate from your life to hear His directions?

2. Vision must be written down

You need a clear vision that belongs to you and directs your life. You cannot be valuable to God's ultimate plan if you do not know and understand your personal vision. Whether you are young, old, married, single, middle-aged, black or white, if you do not have a clearly written vision, the circumstances of life will easily distract, discourage, and disappoint you.

> *"We are all faced with a series of great opportunities brilliantly disguised as impossible situations." Charles Swindoll*

You learned from the first key you have to get alone with God in your personal watchtower to hear from Him. Habakkuk received a vision from God of what would eventually happen to the Babylonians. He did not instruct Habakkuk to think, pray, and talk about the vision, but He specifically told him to write the vision He would reveal. God knew a written vision would solidify it in the hearts and minds of the people.

God's vision is not based upon what you have or do not have. It does not matter what others say or do not say. It does not matter how much money you have or do not have. It does not matter if you are the CEO or the janitor.

You may not totally understand everything God is revealing to you; it may not make much sense, but write it down anyway. What you write down may not match your current situation. What you write down may seem unachievable. What you write down may look crazy to others and even you. You may even second-guess your abilities and talents.

You must believe that if God said it you can take it to the bank and cash it. He may give you a plan to pay off your debt, but you are broke. He may give you a plan for a business, but you do not have the necessary experience. He may give you a plan for a successful marriage, but you are still single.

> **7 Characteristics of a powerful vision**
>
> - *Vision threatens your comfort zone.*
> - *Vision demands change.*
> - *Vision is people oriented.*
> - *Vision is empowering.*
> - *Vision reveals a promising future.*
> - *Vision is given to an individual.*
> - *Vision unfolds progressively.*

Whatever He reveals to you, write it down and start moving toward it.

Today is the right day to begin writing your personal and/or family vision statement. Your vision statement is what God reveals to you and not what you receive from someone's insight, book or seminar. I encourage you to write your vision in explicit details.

Do not leave anything out because you feel inadequate or incapable because of the enormity of the vision. Please know God's vision will be bigger than what you can do or handle in your own strength. His vision can intimidate you. It can make you feel inept and look foolish. Your abilities and skills can look insufficient, but when He reveals your vision to you, it is your responsibility to put it into action.

Why would God tell you to write your vision?

Why is it important for a man to write his vision?

3. Vision must be plain.

> *"... and make it plain upon tables that he may run that reads it..."* Habakkuk 2:2

After spending the necessary time writing your vision, you need to make sure it is written in plain, simple-to-understand language. You want your vision so plain a fifth grader can understand it. I have read complex and convoluted vision statements that left the people assigned to it confused and discouraged because it lacked focus and clear direction.

> *"If you can't fly, then run, If you can't run, then walk, If you can't walk, then crawl, but whatever you do, you have to keep moving forward." Martin Luther King Jr.*

They were well-written statements with impressive and inspirational words and phrases but lacked real direction to motivate people to move. The vision statements were so complicated that the individual with the vision could not really explain it in a way that allowed others to grasp it and run with it.

If you have a vision that is not easily grasped by the people connected to it, they will not follow it and they will end up creating an alternate vision to follow.

When Habakkuk received his vision from God, he wrote it in plain and understandable terms for all the Israelites and future generations to see. The vision he wrote is recorded in scripture to give us a roadmap on how to write a vision statement.

An effective vision statement that is plain and understandable will equip and empower your future generation with the tools they need to excel. When your great-great-great grandchildren read your vision, they will plainly understand its directions and continue to run with it.

We can sometimes over-complicate things because we either think we are smarter than we actually are or we are trying to impress others. A vision statement that is written in plain understandable language will energize and ignite an excitement in everyone connected to it and they will run with eager anticipation.

Why would God tell you to write your vision?

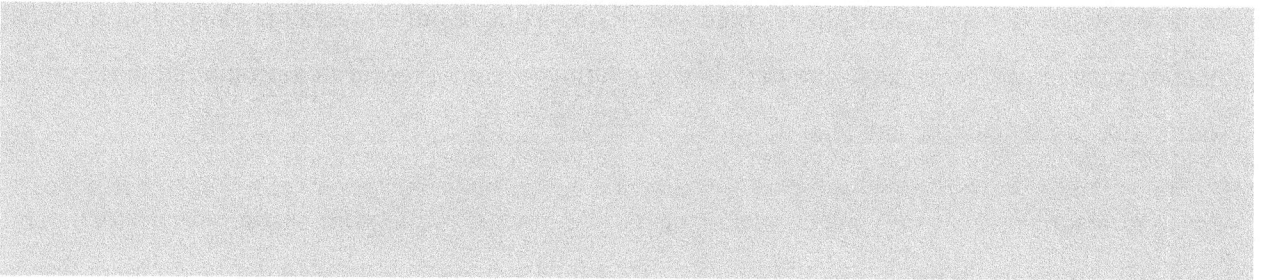

Why is it important for a man to write his vision?

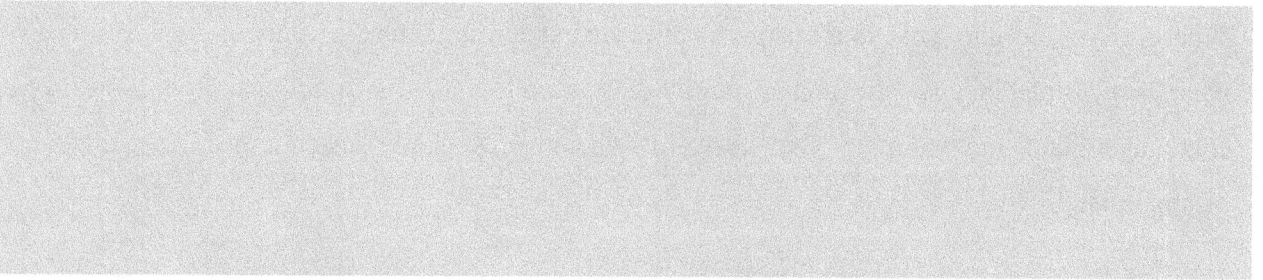

4. Vision must be posted.

"One of the marks of successful people is that they are action-oriented. One of the marks of average people is that they are talk-oriented." Brian Tracy

If you walk into the entrance of some companies and ministries, you will see a posted vision statement. This posted vision statement gives the direction for the organization. Everyone who enters the company or ministry knows that there is a clear and definite direction. Most of all, their posted vision statement gives direction and unifies everyone connected to it. This is very important because it puts everyone on the same page. No one is left in the dark about the direction of the organization.

Just as a business or ministry posts its vision statement, you need to visibly post your vision statement to keep you and everyone connected to it progressing in the same direction. When everyone is on the same page, it brings a greater level of clarity, responsibility and accountability.

> *"The most pathetic person in the world is someone who has sight, but has no vision."*
> *Helen Keller*

After you have written your vision statement in plain understandable terminology, it is now time to post it. I suggest typing it on a one-page summary sheet that you can frame. Once you frame your vision statement, place it in an ideal location visible for you to see every day. If it is a family vision, place it in a prominent place where your entire family can see and read it.

Use it as a screen saver on your computer or mobile device. Write your vision on an index card, laminate it and carry it in your wallet or purse. Post it on your refrigerator so that every time you or someone opens it they will see the vision.

Wherever you need to, post your vision. Your posted vision statement is your constant reminder of what is possible in your life and/or family if you follow God's directions. It becomes your encourager and motivator to live forward whenever you are discouraged, distracted, or disappointed by life.

Why do you believe it is important to post your vision?

Where can you post your vision to keep you and others on track?

5. Vision overcomes obstacles.

"For the vision is yet for the appointed time. It hastens toward the goal and it will not fail. Though it tarries, wait for it. For it will certainly come, it will not delay." Habakkuk 2:3

Do not think because God gives you a clear vision your life is going to be smooth sailing. You will encounter some overwhelming obstacles. You will experience some unforeseeable turbulence. You will have days you want to throw in the towel and walk away from everything.

The enemy will use every tactic in his arsenal to detour your destiny. He will use your friends, family, coworkers, and even you against yourself. His ultimate job is to steal, kill, and destroy your vision (John 10:10).

He will speak discouraging commentary into your ear like, "Don't you know where you come from? No one is going to listen to you.

> *"Too many of us are not living our dreams because we are living our fears."*
> **Les Brown**

You failed the last time… why try again?" The enemy wants you to walk away from your commitments. He wants you to live inconsistently to your purpose. He knows if he can keep you distracted from living your vision's full potential then you will not impact your family, community, and city the way God designed for you.

Not only will the enemy present obstacles to your vision, but others will try to dissuade you from advancing. They will say things like, "How are you going to accomplish that with your education or skill set? That has never been done before in your family. You know you are too old or young to make that happen?" Do not let what others say determine your destiny. Do not let them talk you out of God's promises for your life. Turn a deaf ear to their negative words and focus on your vision.

> *"The way to get started is to quit talking and begin doing." Walt Disney*

You are a major obstacle to living your vision. You and I will talk ourselves out of our vision. We will say what we cannot do instead of saying, "I can do everything God designed me to do." We will say we cannot accomplish something because of our background or lack of experience. Instead, we need to say, "I am going to learn and do what I need to and God will take care of the rest."

When fear and worry attempt to dissuade you, you need to say, "God did not give me the spirit of fear, but of power, love, and a sound mind." (II Timothy 1:7) When you turn your attention in the direction of your vision instead of your problems, you can walk in the assurance that victory is possible.

God designed your life to be motivated and fueled by His vision. You do not have to run and hide from life's challenges. You do not have to live a mediocre existence. You do not have to downplay who you are. You can pursue your vision with an aggressive, offensive attack that will equip and empower you to overcome any obstacles that stand in your way.

What obstacles are present in your life that you have allowed to hinder your vision?

How can you overcome the obstacles to your vision?

6. Vision manifests itself in God's time.

Habakkuk waited patiently for his vision. God revealed that He would use the wicked Babylonians to punish Judah. He would allow the Babylonians to rule for a season, but in due time they would be punished for their wickedness. Habakkuk teaches us the all-important virtue of waiting.

God desires for us to know through Habakkuk's vision that we are to cherish our waiting period. Though it may take a while before your vision unfolds, you are to use your waiting period as a time to grow in knowledge and walk in wisdom. Your waiting period is your proving ground to make the necessary preparations you need because when your vision begins to manifest itself, you want to be ready to operate in it.

Please do not rush your vision. Be patient. When you make your own plans to execute, you force those plans into your own

> *"Our greatest fear should not be of failure but of succeeding at things in life that don't really matter." Francis Chan*

timetable and can possibly delay your destiny. Vision manifests when God determines the time. When the time is right, God will unveil your vision progressively. I know from experience waiting takes patience. The difficulty of patience surfaces when you see the possibilities, but it seems like things are stuck in molasses.

You may have written your vision in explicit detail. You may have followed it to the letter, but it seems nothing is working out. It seems the more you work toward your vision, the more difficult it gets. The more attacks you encounter, the more aggravated and frustrated you become. You may get to the point that you just want to bail out. You want to tell God He can have this vision because it isn't worth the time and energy.

Whether it is going back to school, exercising more days a week, turning off the television and reading or learning a new area at work, you must make the necessary adjustments to bring your vision forth. You are going to have to work on your vision when others are playing, sleeping, and having a good time.

You are going to have to make sacrifices that will cost you something in the short term. Hang in there, because your release is coming soon. You cannot quit when your vision journey becomes a little uncomfortable. You cannot walk away when the road gets bumpy. Just know the finish line is in front of you.

"If you can't fly, then run. If you can't run, then walk. If you can't walk, then crawl, but whatever you do, you have to keep moving forward." Martin Luther King Jr.

Your revealed vision will inspire you to look beyond your waiting process and see your future promise. Now, when I talk about waiting, I am not talking about waiting like at a bus stop. At a bus stop, you just stand waiting on the next bus to arrive. When I talk about waiting, I am talking about waiting like a server at a restaurant.

A good server is constantly moving, serving the customers he is responsible for taking care of. If he wants a good tip, he makes sure his customers are properly served. He does not stop making sure their drinks are filled and their food is properly prepared. He continues to provide excellent service until the customers leave.

The server anticipates that at the end of the meal, if he provided superb service, he stands a great chance of getting an excellent tip. Even if he does not get the tip he thinks he deserves, when the next customer comes, he gives the same excellent service anticipating a good tip. Just as a server is anticipating a good tip from the excellent service he gives, it is crucial we serve in excellence anticipating the rewards of our vision in this present life and the life to come.

Why would God require you to wait on your vision?

Why is waiting sometimes hard? How can you go through your waiting period with confidence that God is going to see you through?

7. Vision is lived by faith.

"Behold, as for the proud one, His soul is not right within him; but the righteous will live by his faith." Habakkuk 2:4

Habakkuk had total faith in the vision God revealed to him. He declared to the people that the God of the universe would spare them from the ruthless reign of the Babylonians. God assured him that the wicked Babylonians, who trusted in their abilities and strengths, would eventually fall (Habakkuk 2:5-20). Habakkuk's job was to keep encouraging the people to live by faith while they waited patiently for the vision to come to pass.

> *"For we live by faith, not by sight."*
> *2 Corinthians 5:7*

If you operate your vision by sight, you will always see the potential problems and pain that may surface. Seeing your problems and pain from a physical viewpoint may cause you to deviate from pursuing your vision. You may see you have more month than money. You may see friends who said they had your back bail on you. You may witness the economy and job market improving for others, but not for you.

Life is full of potential discouraging and depressing circumstances that can keep you living life on the sidelines. When you decide to live your vision by faith, however, you can move from the sidelines to playing in the game.

One definition of vision is seeing farther than your physical eyes can see. It was hard for the people of Judah to see their deliverance when the Babylonians ruthlessly reigned and ruled over them. How could they see a vision of victory while they were encountering tremendous defeat from their enemy? The only way they could possibly see a vision for victory was through the eyes of faith.

> *"God will meet you where you are in order to take you where He wants you to go."*
> *Tony Evans*

If you are enduring difficult times and are discouraged, if you have lost the desire for your vision due to constant struggles or if you have allowed your circumstances to derail you, you must take an active role in regaining your faith for your vision. God gave you a vision so you would trust Him and not just trust what you see. When you begin to see your vision with the eyes of faith, you understand the obstacles you see are only temporary.

Habakkuk realized through the eyes of God's vision that the Babylonians reign was temporary. Though it was going to be a difficult time for the Israelites under the harsh leadership of the Babylonians, they could live through it by faith in God's vision.

Habakkuk was so in tune with his faith that in Habakkuk 3, he praised God for the victory they would eventually experience over the Babylonians. Faith in your vision is paramount because the way you see your vision determines how you think, what you say and when you act.

The more you focus your attention on your vision, the more your faith grows. Taking slow and steady faith steps on your vision journey opens the door for more opportunities for success to come your way.

If you choose instead to walk by fear, you will waste time and energy on activities that take you away from your unique vision course. If you choose to activate your faith, you will courageously move forward in following your promised path to sure vision success.

How are you going to live your vision by faith when your circumstances may paint a different picture?

Why is waiting sometimes hard? How can you go through your waiting period with confidence that God is going to see you through?

God's vision for your life is not based on what resources you currently have or don't have. It doesn't matter what others say or don't say. It's not dependent upon how much money you have or don't have. The only way to realize your vision is to follow God's directions. When God begins to reveal your vision, it will raise a thirst and hunger in you like never before to pursue your vision.

You may not totally understand everything He is revealing to you. It may not make sense, but write it down anyway. What you write down may not match your current situation. What you write down may look unachievable. What you write down may look impossible to others and even to you.

But if God said it, you can take it to the bank and cash it. He may give you a plan to pay off your debt even if you are broke. He may give you a plan for a business even if you don't have the experience. He may give you a plan for a successful future even if your present is in chaos. Whatever He reveals to you, write it down and start moving toward it.

It is time for you to unlock the power of God's vision for your life. It is time to write out a vision plan for your life and family. It is time to move from just talking about your vision to living it.

Why does God require you to work on your vision and not sit like you are waiting at a bus stop?

"Take the first step in faith. You don't have to see the whole staircase, just take the first step."
Dr. Martin Luther King, Jr.

Truth 4

No More Excuses

John 5: 1-15

MAN UP! RISE TO THE CHALLENGE

No More Excuses

"When Jesus saw him lying there, and knew that he had already been a long time in that condition, He said to him, 'Do you wish to get well?'" John 5:6

Many men cannot lead effectively because they spend too much time making excuses. Men, it is time to stop letting excuses control your life and hold you back from living your best life.

Making excuses is a negative attitude that leads to negative action or NO action whatsoever. You have the power within you to stop the negative stronghold that excuses cause in your life. The only way to stop the negative effect of excuses is to make an immediate shift in mindset.

Until you make a shift in mindset, you will continue to make excuses that hinder your progress. A change in mindset is not a one-time deal, but a daily renewing of the mind that keeps excuses from infiltrating your leadership. Even with the most sincere desire to deflect excuses, however, you can still allow them to creep in and take over without you ever noticing.

What mindset shift must you make to overcome excuses?

The Encounter

During Jesus' time, the Pool of Bethesda laid outside the city walls. It was at this pool that Jesus performed a miracle showing that He is greater than any human infirmity and that there is no substitute for faith in God.

The name of the pool, "Bethesda," is Aramaic. It means "House of Mercy." John tells us that a multitude of those who were sick, blind, lame, and withered were waiting for the moving of the waters. (Luke 5:3) The covered colonnades would have provided shade and covering for the disabled who gathered there, but there was another reason for the popularity of the Pool of Bethesda. Legend had it that an angel would come down into the pool and "stir up the water."

"for an angel of the Lord went down at certain seasons into the pool and stirred up the water; whoever then first, after the stirring up of the water, stepped in was made well from whatever disease with which he was afflicted." Luke 5:4

Take responsibility

Excuses men make for not living their vision:

- *I don't believe God can use me.*
- *I don't have enough time.*
- *I don't have enough money.*
- *I didn't have my father in my life.*
- *I don't have the right education or experience.*
- *I am too old or too young.*
- *I didn't come from the right family background.*
- *I made too many mistakes.*

The extent to which you live your vision and achieve your goals depends on you taking responsibility for your life. When Jesus encountered the man at the pool of Bethesda, he was dealing with a 38-year-old destiny killer. His dreams were dashed. His determination was drained. His destiny was dead.

Year after year, he went to the pool hoping to receive his healing, but he always left dejected and disappointed. As soon as the angel agitated the healing waters, someone would beat him to the pool.

"The sick man answered Him, 'Sir, I have no man to put me into the pool when the water is stirred up, but while I am coming, another steps down before me.'" (John 5:7)

This crippling infirmity caused him to miss out on everything life had to offer and left him full of excuses for why he could not live better. He had no hope for the future. He could see no further than his current situation. He merely existed, with no real purpose, vision, or goal. He was stuck doing the same old thing over and over expecting a different result.

Too many men have a habit of blaming others for their circumstances, like the man at the pool did. They say their parents did not support them, the company did not promote them fast enough, the job market did not provide the right opportunities, they did not come from the right background, and the list goes on and on.

You must always accept responsibility for the things you do and the things you fail to do. Even when events outside of your control

> *"Ninety-nine percent of the failures come from people who have the habit of making excuses." George Washington Carver*

occur, you should avoid making excuses and identify the things which you can change to get better results the next time. When you accept responsibility, you take control of your life. Making excuses robs you of your personal power.

You may have to admit that your situation may be a direct result of the choices you made. If you want to live life at maximum capacity, you must take responsibility for where you are, stop blaming others, learn from your mistakes, make any necessary changes, and move forward.

What excuses are currently holding you hostage from living your best life?

What steps do you need to take to overcome the excuses you listed?

Change your focus

When Jesus asked the man "Do you want to be well," He wanted the man to change his focus from his circumstances and focus on Him. You can't fault the man for his hesitancy because for thirty-eight years, his focus was on his infirmity. Now he had someone challenging his focus. Jesus was calling him to break free from a crippling old repetitive mindset.

When you change your focus, you can change your destiny. You can take an ordinary magnifying glass and position it in a way to focus the rays of the sun and it will burn a hole in a board in a few minutes. If those same rays are not focused through the magnifying glass, it will only heat the board significantly.

> *"Concentrate all your thoughts upon the work at hand. The sun's rays do not burn until brought to a focus."*
> *Alexander Graham Bell*

When the rays of the sun are focused through that magnifying glass, they can do what they cannot do unfocused. Just imagine the power your personal vision can have in your life and the lives of those connected to you when it is focused on what is possible for you.

Why does focus matter so much? With focus, distractions are kept to a minimum and your days are spent in meaningful ways. You regain control over your life and no longer feel like you are wasting time. You ultimately stop going in circles and get on the right path to living your God-designed life.

Each of us has the same 24 hours a day and 168 hours a week. The key questions you should ask yourself are, "Where am I focusing my time?" and "Is it where I need to focus?" If you cannot give definitive answers to these questions, then you may need to refocus.

What repetitive cycle do you need to destroy that is causing you to lose focus?

What past failures or successes have kept you from moving forward?

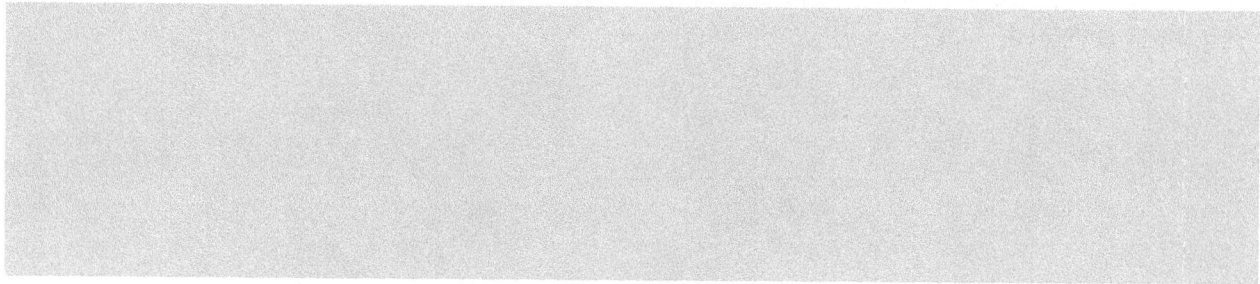

Develop a support team

The man at the pool's acquaintances and circumstances conditioned him to focus on his infirmity. His friends at the pool were in the same, and in some cases worse condition than he was. His friends were like him: They had become conditioned to their circumstances. His family and friends constantly reminded him of his status. He had no one to encourage or challenge him to go after his dreams. He had no one to tell him that he could overcome his circumstances. He had no one in his corner.

> *"Two are better off than one, because together they can work more effectively. If one of them falls down, the other can help him up..." Ecclesiastes 4:9*

Think about the people who are supportive or would be supportive of your vision if you told them. Surround yourself with people who lift you up, not those who drag you down. If you want to do great things in life, you need to surround yourself with a strong support system. You must connect with people who will support your vision and who will be a listening ear.

There will always be people who tell you what you can't do. They will provide the statistics and data that will discourage you from living your dreams. And then there is that little voice inside of your own head that asks "What am I doing? I should throw in towel." or "I will fail because I am not good enough". Don't listen to them! Believe in yourself. Visualize your success and persevere.

Don't let anyone or anything keep you from living your authentic life. You know whose you are. You know what you want. You know it's in your heart to create an extraordinary life for yourself and those connected to you. So go for it.

What people do you need to disconnect from and what people do you need to connect with? How will disconnecting from hindering people and connecting with encouraging people help you move forward?

Take immediate action

The man at the pool looked as if he was stuck in a no-win situation. You may be able to relate to his situation because you are in, or have been in, a similar situation, or you know a man who is. I want to encourage you that there is a way out of your stuck situation. It does not matter if you have been stuck for a year, 5 years, 10 years or 38 years; there is a way out.

All hope looked lost for this man because nothing had changed in his life for 38 years. For 38 years, he missed his healing. For 38 years, life passed him by. For 38 years, he felt like a failure; helpless and stuck. His back was against the wall, with no help in sight.

Even though this man's condition looked hopeless, Jesus knew his condition. He knew the man thought this was the way he was

> *If God is calling you to move in your vision, tell Him yes because He knows what He placed in you to accomplish His will.*

going to live the rest of his life. You may ask: if God knew his situation, why did He wait so long? I cannot answer that, but I can tell you God's timing is the right time. I can tell you, "He will never leave nor forsake you." (Hebrews 11:5) Don't ever think God does not know your situation. Don't think He has forgotten you. Trust me. He knows your location.

When Jesus confronted the man, notice He did not ask him if he wanted to be healed from his infirmity. He asked him, "Do you want to be made whole?" He did not just want the man healed physically, but He wanted the man to be made completely whole. Jesus knew if he received just a physical healing, he still would have been incomplete. He desired for the man to be completely whole, from the inside out. But, in order for the man to receive his healing, he had to take action.

"Jesus said to him, 'Get up, pick up your pallet and walk.' Immediately the man became well, and picked up his pallet and began to walk." John 6: 8-9

Jesus gave him simple instructions to take action. He did not have to seek advice from his friends, get more prayers or discuss his condition. He just had to act upon Jesus's words. When he took action, he was healed.

> *"We cannot solve our problems with the same thinking we used when we created them." Albert Einstein*

Focus on what you can do in the present moment. Don't worry about what you should have done last week or what you might be able to do tomorrow. The only time you can affect is the present. If you focus too much on the past or the future, you won't get anything done today.

Do you want to start exercising? Do you have a great business idea? Do want to change careers? Eliminate the things you do from day to day that distract you from taking action, such as TV, social media, and listening to naysayers. Take action now. The longer you hold on to an idea without taking action, the weaker it becomes and the more power you give to the naysayers, doubters and haters.

It is time to stop making excuses and take action. Conditions may not be ideal to move forward, but usually they are not ideal. You cannot afford to keep waiting for the optimal conditions because if you do, you will miss your opportunity to shine. Choose today to take action.

What has hindered you from taking actions on a goal or dream that you want to accomplish?

What actions have you avoided that you must immediately take toward accomplishing the dream or goal you named?

Expect challenges

When you stop making excuses and begin to take action steps toward living a better life, you will be met with challenges. People who were with you when you were struggling with life will walk away when you start living a better life. People you thought would celebrate and support your turnaround will question your motives.

Instead of the leaders celebrating with the man over his healing, they questioned who delivered him. They were so attached to their traditions that they could not

> *"Others can stop you temporarily; you are the only one who can do it permanently." Zig Ziglar*

appreciate that a man who was crippled for 38 was miraculously healed. They were only concerned that this healing was a violation of their law of working on the Sabbath.

"Now it was the Sabbath on that day. So the Jews were saying to the man who was cured, 'It is the Sabbath, and it is not permissible for you to carry your pallet.'" John 5:10

Has there been a time in your life that you overcame a tough situation and you thought that certain people would celebrate with you, but they turned on you? How did it make you feel? What did you do about it?

Almost nothing worthwhile in life comes without a fight. Challenges are an essential part of life which should be embraced, engaged and overcome as they allow you to grow as a person. Whether you like it or not, you will face challenges along the way, so you might as well avoid making excuses and get on with the job of overcoming them.

Excuses won't get you anywhere at all. Instead, they are terrible distractions that take your focus off of your most important tasks and reduce your confidence and belief. Avoid making excuses and face your challenges head-on. You will be more empowered, more confident, and more successful.

Even when you are met with difficult challenges, how will you move forward with your vision when you know God has shown you what to do?

91

If you want to get from where you are currently in life to where you want to be, you need to avoid making excuses and focus on the tasks that are going to get you there. If excuses were currency, we would all be rich. All the excuses that we make provide nothing of value. Instead, they strip you of your confidence, courage, and creativity to meet your challenges with the expectation of victory.

Your life may have been in a slump far too long. You know deep inside that you should be farther than you currently are. You have a dream inside of you, but you have no idea how to

> **The Effect of Excuses**
> - *Excuses sidetrack men from realizing their vision.*
> - *Excuses silence men's leadership voice.*
> - *Excuses suppress men from living their values.*
> - *Excuses sabotages men's vitality.*
> - *Excuses steal men's victory.*

bring it to the surface. You keep sitting by your pool hoping someone will put you in so that you receive your breakthrough. You may have become like the man at the pool: you have waited by your pool for so long that you are comfortable in your dead-end situation.

You must see yourself living a better today. You must see yourself walking in authority. You must see yourself owning it, using it, living it and walking in it. If you live with a negative mindset full of excuses, then you will lock yourself out of receiving God's bountiful blessings.

If God promised that you can reach your vision, then it is possible. Your responsibility is to believe that it is possible, and then go after it. You don't know what you can accomplish until you stop making excuses and move toward it. You cannot afford to sit on your vision choosing to make the same lame excuses you made yesterday. You cannot continue to watch other men get their breakthrough while you sit looking from the sidelines.

You cannot continue to blame your parents, background, job, or spouse for the fact that your dreams have become nightmares. You must make life-changing decisions to move in a different direction. Like Jesus told the man at the pool, "Get up, pick up your pallet and walk" (John 5:8). I am telling you that today you can get up, pick up your bed, and walk toward your destiny.

Like the man at the pool, you and I can no longer allow excuses to hold us hostage from living our designed destiny. When God gives you a vision, then He can bring that vision to pass through you. Whatever God orders, He can pay for it.

No matter the assignment God is calling you to, you need to jump up and tell Him yes. Do exactly what He tells you. I don't care if it has not been done before; do it anyway. I don't care if no one will go with you, go anyway. I don't care if you don't get the encouragement from others, encourage yourself. I don't care if you do not have the right words to speak, speak His Word. God is waiting for you to answer yes to His call.

Reflection: What one significant thing could you accomplish in your life in the next 12 months if you would stop making excuses and do it? How would accomplishing this significant thing make your life and/or family better?

"The person who really wants to do something finds a way; the other person finds an excuse."
Author Unknown

Truth 5
Values Count

Genesis 39

Values Count

"But he refused and said unto his master's wife. Behold with me here, my master does not concern himself with anything in the house and he has put all that he owns in my charge." Genesis 39:8

In America we have become a society of instant gratification. If things don't happen the way we want we easily give up. If someone does not do things exactly the way we want him/her to do it, we will walk away. Many men are committed to living their values just as long as it is easy and beneficial to them. Men forfeit awesome blessings in their lives when they choose not to commit to their values because things do not go their way.

> **What are Values?**
>
> *Values are deeply held beliefs that certain qualities are desirable. They define what is right or fundamentally important to each of us. They provide guidelines for your choices and actions.*

Joseph is the model example of a man who was committed to living out his values. He made an unwavering commitment to follow his values in spite of strong temptation. He was determined to not let anyone or anything come against him living out his values.

When Potiphar's wife made her moves on Joseph, he did not succumb under the intense pressure to satisfy his flesh. His commitment fortified him to resist her daily sexual advancements. He didn't care how good she looked or that he might have gotten away with it. He knew God had entrusted him with an awesome vision and he wasn't going to follow his flesh and give into her temptations.

Joseph understood that a few moments of pleasure could wreck his future. His main concern was not Potiphar finding out, but that he would be sinning against God. Joseph stood fast on his promise, but his refusal to lie with Potiphar's wife did not stop her advancements; it only intensified them. The scripture emphasizes that she pressured him day after day to lie with her, but Joseph kept singing the same song; I cannot lie with you and forfeit my promise. *"As she spoke to Joseph day after day, he did not listen to her to lie beside her or be with her."* (Genesis 39:10).

Have you ever forfeited something of value for a few minutes of pleasure? How did it make you feel afterward? Was the pleasure worth the sacrifice? Describe what you would do differently if that pleasure presented itself again?

Potiphar's wife used Joseph's rejections as fuel for her burning desire to lie with him. She wasn't going to accept no for an answer. She pursued him day after day, and every day he avoided her advances, until one day she became more aggressive and grabbed him.

"Now it happened one day that he went into the house to do his work, and none of the men of the household was there inside. She caught him by his garment, saying, 'Lie with me!' And he left his garment in her hand and fled, and went outside." Genesis 39:11-12

I love what Joseph did next: instead of giving in to her advances, he ran. Men, we need to follow Joseph's example. When we are pressured to forfeit our commitment to our values, we need to do a 180-degree turn and run. Sometimes merely trying to avoid temptation is not enough. You must turn and run, understanding that the temptation is too great for you to stand against it.

What would you have done in a similar situation as Joseph? Would you have given into the temptation or would you have held faithful to your core values?

97

What current temptations are you struggling with that is coming against you and everything you value? What are you doing to avoid this temptation? Who can you ask to hold you accountable to overcoming this temptation?

There are many temptations that want to sidetrack you from living out your values. There is material temptation, which is the lust for things. Men will work 50 and 60 hour weeks for years because of their lust for material things. They will surrender their relationships with their spouse, children and friends because they are pursuing some shiny object that they think will bring them satisfying pleasure. They soon discover after getting the shiny object that it truly does not bring the pleasure they were seeking, so they will go after something else thinking it will satisfy them.

> *Your core values determine what is really important to you. When you make the decision to follow your core values you cannot be easily persuaded to live against them.*

There is personal pleasure temptation, which is the lust for fame, authority, control and power. It may be as simple as lusting for a position at work, church or in the community. It may be the desire to be in authority over people. Some men will undercut and roll over others to get a position or title that they think will give them power and prestige. Men will use their position to dominate their spouses and children for the sake of control.

And then there is sensual temptation, which is the lust for another person. Many men find themselves intensely struggling with this temptation. We hear countless stories of men throwing away years of significant gains for a few moments of pleasure. Men will sacrifice their values and ruin their reputations just to fulfill their lustful fleshly appetites.

Joseph engaged in this battle with Potiphar's wife. She lusted for Joseph, but Joseph refused to give into his flesh. He chose to be faithful to his core values. His core values became the filter through which he determined right from wrong, significant from insignificant, and purpose from pleasure. Though following his core values cost him a few moments of pleasure, he understood that God had a greater vision for his life.

What values have been present in your life since childhood?

To become effective in your life's journey, you need to identify and develop clear and concise core values. Your core values are central in defining who you are, what you do and where you go. Once defined, your core values should guide you in every aspect of your daily life.

When you make a conscious decision to follow your core values, you cannot be easily persuaded to live against them. It is

> *"Strive for integrity – that means knowing your values in life and behaving in a way that is consistent with these values."*

these core values that determine what is really important to you as a man. The surprising thing is that if you ask most men what their core values are, many would not be able to give you a solid answer.

Some would give you a list of values, but they would not be able to prioritize them. They will give you a list that sounds spiritual or politically correct, but they don't come close to living them. In order to live the vision God designed for you effectively, you must have a set of prioritized core values that guides your daily life.

In order for you to live your core values even under extreme temptation, your core values should be:

1. Clearly Stated

You should have a set of clearly stated and prioritized core values that guide your daily life. When you don't know or you haven't clearly defined your values, you end up drifting along in life. Instead of basing your decisions on an internal compass, you make choices based on circumstances and social pressures. You end up trying to fulfill other people's expectations instead of your own. And before you know it, life has passed you by and you haven't even started to live.

> *"If we did all the things we are capable of doing, we would literally astound ourselves."*
> *Thomas Edison*

Trying to be someone else and living without core values is downright exhausting and leaves you feeling empty and frustrated. Conversely, living a life in line with your core values brings purpose, direction, joy and peace.

While facing the constant sexual advancements of Potiphar's wife, Joseph held true to his core value to God. He told her,

"There is no one greater in this house than I, and he has withheld nothing from me except you, because you are his wife. How then could I do this great evil and sin against God?" Genesis 39:9

I have noticed that when I take the time to really think and meditate upon what I value as a man and then write those things down, I'm more likely to have the courage and confidence to make choices based on those values. There's something about actually writing down your values that makes you more committed to living them.

Why is clearly stating your core values important?

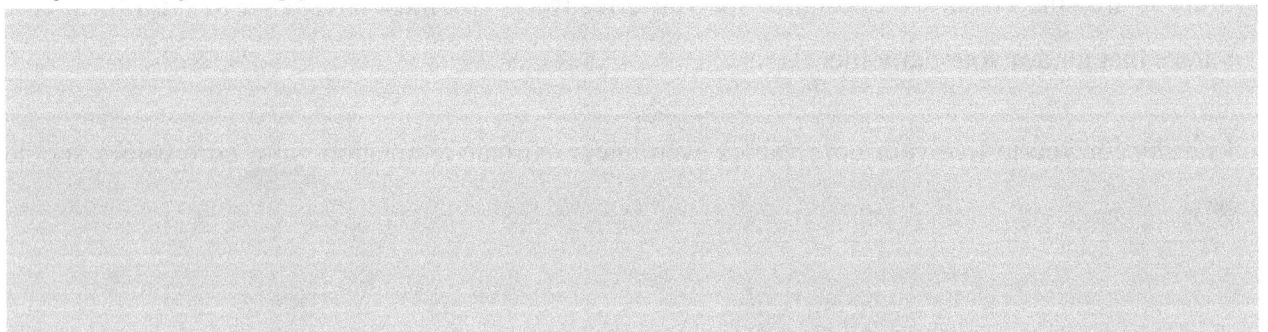

Reflect on your lifestyle and how you spend your time. How well does your life reflect your core values?

2. Conscientiously Chosen

Your core values should be in direct agreement with your purpose. It's not enough to *say* something is a core value it needs to have an active influence over your behavior and actions. This is what learning to live on purpose is all about. For this very reason, it's absolutely critical that you explore your personal values in detail in order to pinpoint what it is you value most.

> *"If we are to go forward, we must go back and rediscover those precious values--that all reality hinges on moral foundations and that all reality has spiritual control."*
> *Martin Luther King, Jr.*

This will help you find the right balance to live your life based on your highest priorities. When you come to understand your values, you can use them to make better decisions about your life and circumstances. This is advantageous because it can help you decide with more clarity what kind of career you should pursue, how you should spend your money, what kind of relationship you should search for, what people to connect with, where to take risks, what business to start and which goals to pursue. Joseph's value-focused living allowed his purpose to prosper in the house of Potiphar. Genesis 39:1-4 brings to focus what can happen when you conscientiously live out your values.

"The LORD was with Joseph, so he became a successful man. And he was in the house of his master, the Egyptian. [3] Now his master saw that the LORD was with him and how the LORD caused all that he did to prosper in his hand. [4] So Joseph found favor in his sight and became his personal servant; and he made him overseer over his house, and all that he owned he put in his charge."

Conscientiously choosing your values is very important because your values determine what you focus on, how you perceive reality, how you evaluate things, and what you will or won't do, which essentially comes down to your behavior and the actions you take on a daily basis. If your values are not aligned with your daily decisions, choices, and actions, then you will miss the mark of living your vision with power.

Name 5 to 7 important values in your life. Prioritize these values.

Do your core values line up with God's values (Galatians 5:22-23)? If not, what do you need to do to make sure your values are in line with God's values?

3. Committed Daily

There are numerous definitions for the word commitment. The most basic definition is that commitment is a binding agreement between the heart, mind and emotions that puts a man on a course of action toward living out his values. When you really commit to living your values, you will not allow the distractions of the world's false promises to detour you.

Commitment to living your values is something that just doesn't happen because you talk about it or write it down. It doesn't progress because you

> *"It's not hard to make decisions when you know what your values are."*
> *Roy E. Disney*

say you want to accomplish a certain goal. It doesn't happen because you follow your values for a week or two. Commitment is tested by your daily actions and not your words. If you have a job, then you should value doing the best that you can do while you are there. If you are married, you should value being a faithful and loving husband.

If you are a father, you should value training your children in a Godly manner. You should value being a lifelong learner and making yourself better on a daily basis. Part of becoming the man God desires for you to be is staying committed to living your values at all costs.

Joseph was committed to living his values and was willing to make an unwavering commitment to follow his vision even under adverse circumstances. Even as Potiphar's wife tempted him daily with enticing words, he did not succumb.

"As she spoke to Joseph day after day, he did not listen to her to lie beside her or be with her."
Genesis 39:10

When men authentically commit to living their values, they won't let anyone or anything detour their progress. They won't let the economy or the job market drain their energy. They won't allow failure and doubt to hinder their journey. They will make a commitment from the heart and determine not to succumb to the intense pressures to give up, give in, or quit. Commitment is not something that happens because you dream of it.

Commitment is tested by your daily actions and not your words. If you have a job then you should commit to doing the very best that you can while you are there. If you are married you should commit to being a faithful and loving husband or wife. If you are a father or mother, you should commit to training your children in a Godly manner. If you want to grow in knowledge and wisdom, you must be committed to being a lifelong learner.

What commitments have you struggled to keep? What do you need to do to remain committed even through struggles?

Reflection: Discuss a time in your life when you made a promise to commit to something, but after a short time your commitment fizzled out? What would you do differently?

4. Consistently Followed

You are responsible for consistently living your core values on a daily basis. Determine what is worth dying for and then make that the basis for your decisions. You cannot afford to waste another day not being committed to your vision. If you are like me, you have wasted enough time and energy being inconsistent. Your vision is screaming for your consistency. Your family is crying out for your consistency. Those that are connected to you that you haven't met or never will meet need your consistency.

Because you commit to living your vision with consistency, do not automatically think everything is going to fall into place. Don't think everyone that is close to you will support your efforts. Don't believe that you are not going to encounter some struggles. Sometimes the exact opposite happens. Your life may get more chaotic. Things that used to work stop working. Individuals who said they were going to be with you leave you hanging. That does not mean you give up. It may mean that you are on the right track to living out your commitments.

One of the difficult things to reconcile in Joseph's story is that even though he lived his values consistently, Potiphar's wife falsely

> *"If a man hasn't discovered something that he will die for, he isn't fit to live."*
> *Martin Luther King, Jr.*

accused him of attempted rape. And from this false accusation Joseph was thrown in prison.

"Now when his master heard the words of his wife, which she spoke to him, saying, 'This is what your slave did to me,' his anger burned. So Joseph's master took him and put him into the jail, the place where the king's prisoners were confined; and he was there in the jail. Genesis 39:19-20

This goes to show that even though you live your values consistently, bad things can still happen. But even though bad things can happen, you must still keep your focus on God and the values he desires for you to live out. God has not forgotten you. Romans 8:28 says, *"And we know that God causes all things to work together for good to those who love God, to those who are called according to His purpose."*

When you read the rest of Joseph's story (Genesis 39-41), you will see all the benefits he reaped from consistently living his values. God eventually raised him from the prison to the palace. It may look scary and intimidating because you are about to move from lip service to action, giving up to rising up, defeat to victory and ordinary to extraordinary. You may realize what you have been missing all this time is **True Consistency**.

What distractions are present around you that interfere with you living your values consistently?

How can you become more consistent in living out your values?

5. Constantly Evaluated

You should constantly evaluate your values to make sure you don't need to reprioritize them or make adjustments. It's important to note that your values will often change as you transition through different life stages.

Major life events can also change your values. For instance, a close family member passing away can shift how you think about your life, your path and how you think about others. This can change how you prioritize things and how you live your life. There are many life changes that can shift how you prioritize your values. For instance, your values will be different while you are in college, after you get married, have children or get older. Events such as these can shift how you think about things and how you prioritize your values.

Joseph's life was constantly changing. He went from realizing his purpose to being thrown in a pit to living in Potiphar's house to being thrown in prison to becoming the Pharaoh's top leader. His core values kept him faithful to God during all these major swings in life. He kept God's favor because he refused to live against his values. Even in the most difficult situations, he lived true to his values and continually found favor with God.

"But the LORD was with Joseph and extended kindness to him, and gave him favor in the sight of the chief jailer." Genesis 39:21

"Pharaoh said to Joseph, 'See, I have set you over all the land of Egypt.'" Genesis 41:41

> **"How much better it is to get wisdom than gold and to get understanding is to be chosen above silver." Proverbs 16:16**

Keeping track of your values is a great way to stay in-tune with your deepest needs and desires. What was once important may not be important any longer. As a result, you must alter your choices and decisions in order to match your highest values and priorities. Failing to take these steps can leave you feeling unbalanced, dissatisfied and unfulfilled.

There will, of course, be some values that will stay constant throughout your life. These could be values connected to your relationship with God, wife and children, your physical and mental health and financial stability. These core values are the values that determine how you live your life from the deepest recesses of your heart. These values will rarely change and are often ingrained in your psyche at a very young age.

Which value is the most important that you absolutely cannot live without? Why is this value so important?

There is no right or wrong way to document your core values and there is no magic number you should have. What is important is that you choose the right values for you and your family and you live by them daily. You should live by your values even when your life is in a season of confusion. You should live by your values when other men are not living theirs. You should live by your values when the enemy is telling you it is fine to live the way you want because other men are doing their own thing.

Once you establish your core values and start living them, watch your life begin to turn in a different and more progressive direction. Don't get frustrated and quit living your core values if it seems difficult, but keep praying, believing and moving through the process.

Would you give up a job, friends, monetary gain, prestige and power to live your values? Why would you give up any of these things? Why might it be hard to give up any of these things?

What are you doing right now to model and to teach your core values to your children and future generations? How well does your life reflect your core value?

"It's not hard to make decisions when you know what your values are."
Roy E. Disney

Truth 6
Moses Is Dead

Joshua 1

Moses Is dead

"Moses My servant is dead; now therefore arise, cross this Jordan, you and all this people, to the land which I am giving to them, to the sons of Israel." Joshua 1:2

Joshua is considered one of the Bible's greatest military leaders and he is often regarded as a model for effective leadership. Joshua is best known as Moses' second in command who takes over and leads the Israelites into the Promised Land after Moses' death. Joshua was groomed for this role since they left Egypt for their journey to the Promised Land. He was one of the twelve men that Moses selected to spy out the Promised Land. When Joshua returned to report on the land, his conviction was strong that God would help them take back the land (Numbers 14).

"The real tragedy in life is not death, but to let your vision die inside of you while you still live." Bernard Haynes

The Lord selected Joshua to be Moses' successor long before Moses' death. Then He commissioned Joshua the son of Nun, and said, "Be strong and courageous, for you shall bring the sons of Israel into the land which I swore to them, and I will be with you." (Deut. 31:23) Joshua had some big shoes to fill. God had chosen him to lead His people against the enemies in the Promised Land.

Moses led the Children of Israel for more than forty years. He led them out of Egyptian bondage. He led them on dry ground through the Red Sea. He interceded on their behalf when they abandoned God's instructions. Moses led them through extreme circumstances, gave them the Ten Commandments from God, and taught and governed the people. The Children of Israel grew up knowing only Moses as their leader. Now Moses was dead.

What would they do? Would their enemies defeat them? How could they inherit the Promised Land without Moses? God had a leader that He would use to do an incredible work. Joshua was his man. You may wonder, how can I lead with my negative past? Will my family support me? How can I lead effectively when I have failed so many times?

There has been a time in every man's life that he has felt insufficient, inadequate and incapable of leading. You can learn from the life of Joshua in the Book of Joshua how you can take the reins of leadership that God has assigned to your life. In this chapter, you will study five keys from the first chapter of Joshua that will help you put yesterday in the rearview mirror and live your today with high expectations.

1. Leave the Past in the Past

God reminded Joshua that although Moses had been a great man and a great leader who led the Children of Israel out of Egypt into freedom, as long as Moses was alive, the children of Israel could not enter the Promised Land. The Lord had

> *"When one door closes another door opens; but we so often look so long and so regretfully upon the closed door, that we do not see the ones which open for us." Alexander Graham Bell*

told Moses that because of his disobedience in striking the rock instead of speaking to the rock in the wilderness, he would be permitted to view the land, but not walk into it.

"But the LORD said to Moses and Aaron, 'Because you have not believed Me, to treat Me as holy in the sight of the sons of Israel, therefore you shall not bring this assembly into the land which I have given them.'" Numbers 20:12

If you desire to take hold of your destiny, the first thing you must do is leave your failures and regrets in the past. Your past is like scrambled eggs and you can't unscramble them. Whatever happened in your past, deal with it so you can move on. Don't spend another minute stressed out over something you can't change. Don't let your past hold you hostage from achieving your dreams. Don't let your mistakes define who you are or what you can do. Don't let others negative views dictate how you live your life.

Why do you believe it was important for God to stress to Joshua that Moses was dead?

You have endured intense struggles and overcome insurmountable obstacles, so you can't afford to allow your failures and regrets to bind you to the past. When you stay locked in the past, you become stuck and unable to progress forward. We all have failures and regrets that we are ashamed of and many have cost us great pain, heartache and loss. You cannot go back and redo what happened, but you can forgive yourself or seek forgiveness from others and move on with your life.

Moses is gone and will never come back. Maybe you have not achieved what you envisioned because you are still tied to yesterday. In order to move

> *"Don't let fear bind you to the past so you don't respond in faith to your present." Bernard Haynes*

forward and realize what God has for you, it is important that you say good-bye to yesterday (Moses). Whatever happened in your past is a part of your life that you will never get back. Use your yesterday to improve today and live a better tomorrow.

What past failure or regret that is hindering your progress do you need to let go of?

You cannot live a better today if you are stuck on what happened yesterday. What you should or could have done yesterday is a fleeting memory. You can't turn back the hands of time. Your moment is right now. If you don't do what you need to do today, then today will eventually become yesterday and you will miss another chance.

Don't miss doing what you need to do today because you are still focused on what didn't happen yesterday. It is time for you to put your past behind you. Let your past go and live in the present moment. Envision a brighter future ahead of you. You can't give in or succumb to your past failures and regrets because your best life is waiting for you to live it.

113

What's keeping you tied to the failure of regret? What action can you take to finally let it go?

2. Rise up

After God told Joshua that Moses was dead, He then told him to rise up and cross over the Jordan. He did not tell him to pray about it, talk about it or get someone else's opinion about it. He told him to take action. You can't get anything done sitting on your butt. Talking about your vision won't make it happen. Telling others about it won't bring it to pass. Dreaming about it won't manifest it. You must take consistent action daily to birth your vision.

> *"A hero is an ordinary individual who finds the strength to persevere and endure in spite of overwhelming obstacles."*
> *Christopher Reeve*

Life is too short and unpredictable to keep dreaming and talking about what you need and desire to do. The only way you and I can move in a different direction is to take action. Without action, you miss living the vision God designed for you.

If Joshua had sat around crying about Moses, dwelling on yesterday or talking about what they could do, he and the Children of Israel would have missed out on their promise. They had to accept that change was at hand.

Life is constantly about change; it is forever moving. Yesterday seems light-years away. Don't waste any more time agonizing over what happened yesterday. Don't let yesterday's setbacks keep you from living today's opportunities. If you hit unforeseen turbulence, don't quit. If you don't succeed at first, don't throw in the towel. Change your course and go in a different direction.

Are your daily actions bringing you closer to where you desire to be? If not, what must you do to get where you need to be?

Getting where you desire to be takes effort. You must roll up your sleeves, strap on your work boots, put on your hardhat and go to work.

Reading books about others' success won't magically transfer success to you. Listening to motivational message after motivational message won't bring instant success. You must conclude that you if you are going to live your best life, you must choose to change your mindset, create a plan and consistently take action.

Don't be a one-hit wonder who takes action one time and thinks everything will fall into place without taking action again. Don't miss your

> *"You don't know how strong you really are until being strong is the only choice you have." Bernard Haynes*

opportunity waiting for something magical to happen, for the right person to show up, for the perfect situation to come or for your past to go away. Rise up, seek God's face, take consistent action, and watch what happens.

You make the choice whether you stay where you are or rise up and take action. If you are like me, you cannot afford to stay where you are. Life is too fragile and unpredictable to remain locked in a comfortable pain. It is time to break free of the pains of yesterday and the chains of regret and take a leap of faith.

In order for Joshua and the Children of Israel to possess the Promised Land, they had to go and get what God had already given them. They had to get up. If Joshua had stayed where he was and never got up to cross over the Jordan River, he and the Israelites would have never received their promise.

What promises are you missing out on because you are afraid to get up and make a move?

How can Joshua's success story help you rise above your circumstances and take action?

It is not going to be easy. The lure of comfortability is powerful. Jumping off the edge presents danger. It requires doing something you have never done before, and doing it without all the answers. You must trust the vision God gave you.

The negative thoughts will ring loud like a rock band at a concert. Every time you attempt to move forward, the decibels of negativity grow louder. The more you move toward rising up and taking that leap of faith, the more complacency and stagnation will pull you back.

Your negative inner voice will say, "What are you doing?" "Who will support you?" "You failed the last three times," "You do not know the right people," or "You do not have the right education or skill set," and the list goes on and on. Your negative inner voice will discourage and deflate you to the point that you stay stuck where you are.

I can only imagine what the negative inner voice of Joshua was saying. It may have said, "You know the people are not going to listen to you," "You cannot lead like Moses," or "You are going to fail." I am glad that Joshua did not listen to the negative inner voice and instead allowed the voice of God to be the prominent voice in his life. God knew that the task of possessing the Promised Land would not be easy for Joshua and the Israelites. So He encouraged Joshua with words of what was possible if he would rise up and walk in faith.

> *"Stop wasting time on things that don't matter and people who don't think you matter." Bernard Haynes*

"Every place on which the sole of your foot treads, I have given it to you, just as I spoke to Moses. From the wilderness and this Lebanon, even as far as the great river, the river Euphrates, all the land of the Hittites, and as far as the Great Sea toward the setting of the sun will be your territory. No man will be able to stand before you all the days of your life. Just as I have been with Moses, I will be with you; I will not fail you or forsake you." (Joshua 1:2-5)

You do not have to spend another second, minute, hour, day, week, month or year held hostage by fear. Today you can experience everything that awaits you. Rise up. Take a leap of faith and start living out your vision. Don't worry. Don't fear. Don't doubt. God has your back.

Does your negative inner voice speak to you when you are ready to make a faith move? What does it say? How can you quiet your negative inner voice and move to where God is directing you?

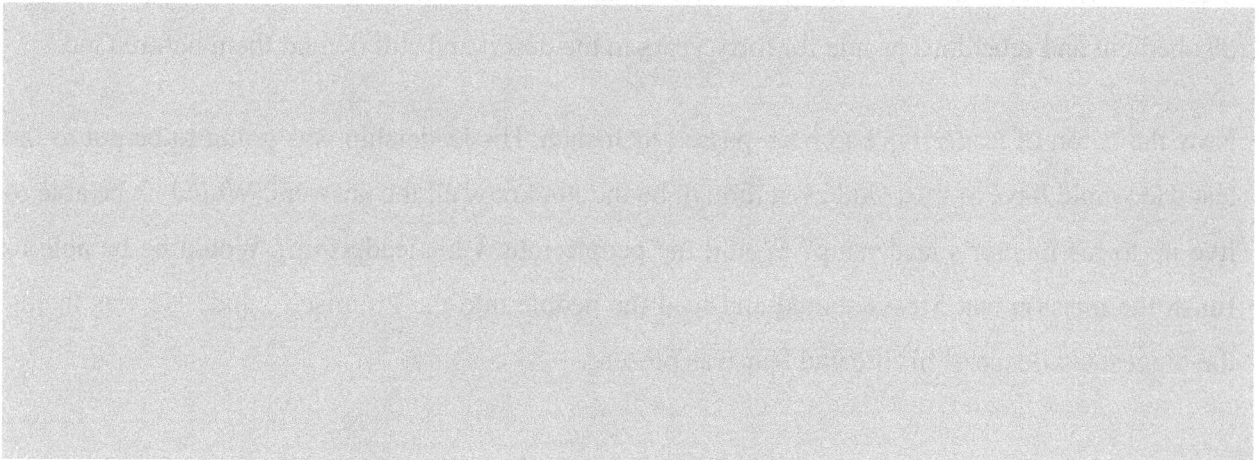

How can you trust God even though you cannot see how things will work out?

3. Possess real courage

Courage is standing when everyone else wants to run, speaking when everyone is afraid to speak, acting when everyone is paralyzed by fear, taking action in the face of danger, holding one's character and moral uprightness when everyone else is tempted to compromise theirs.

Joshua was overcome with fear as he encountered the biggest transition of his life. Moses was dead and he was next in charge. He was about to begin his reign as the leader of the Israelites. The man who boldly told Moses they could defeat the inhabitants in the Promised Land was now dealing with fear.

> *"Be strong and of good courage, do not fear nor be afraid of them; for the LORD your God, He is the One who goes with you. He will not leave you nor forsake you."*
> *Deuteronomy 31:6*

Joshua's fear is certainly understandable. He was not following any ordinary leader; he was following in the footsteps of Israel's greatest leader. He saw Moses part the Red Sea. He was present when Moses delivered the Ten Commandments from Mount Sinai. He saw Moses lead a disobedient and rebellious people for forty years in the desert and still defend them before God.

Now the baton of leadership had been passed to Joshua. His leadership was going to be put to the test. He would have to trust God even though he did not know all the answers. Would he be able to live up to his mentor's leadership? Would the people follow his leadership? Would he be able to finish the mission that Moses started and lead the people into the Promised Land? He was facing the biggest challenge of his life and fear was present.

What fears are you struggling with?

How can you overcome the fears you named?

Change always produces fear! That is why we can all identify with Joshua. When we don't know what is going to happen or how things are going to work out, it naturally causes fear to stir our hearts.

Trusting in God is our ultimate remedy for fear, yet that sometimes seems easier said than done. In fact, the more consumed with fear we become, the more distant God seems to be. That's why, when anxiety grips your heart, you should make a concerted effort to stand on the promises of God's Word, claim them over your life, and then walk with courage.

God gave Joshua a powerful word that he could hold onto. The words God poured into Joshua equipped him to walk in courage and not let fear

> *"Courage is the mastery of fear, not the absence of fear." Mark Twain*

direct him. God repeatedly told Joshua to be strong and courageous. This phrase became the mantra of Joshua's life and gave him the strength to continuously move forward.

"Be strong and courageous, for you shall give this people possession of the land which I swore to their fathers to give them. [7] Only be strong and very courageous; be careful to do according to all

119

the law which Moses My servant commanded you; do not turn from it to the right or to the left, so that you may have success wherever you go." Joshua 1: 6-7

If you desire to overcome the spirit of fear, you must trust God to keep His word. Rely on His ability to take care of the source of your fears. You must rest in God and His word and allow Him to take over solving your challenges.

Many men never fulfill the call of God on their lives simply because, every time they try to go forward, the enemy uses fear to stop them. Is he using fear to stop you?

Do you have a scripture from God that keeps you moving forward? If not, what scripture can you adopt as your mantra from God's Word that you can use in your life?

4. Seize your moment

There are moments in life when you have to overcome fear and exercise faith. When your moment comes, you can't wait to see who is going to go with you. You can't wait for things in your life to be perfect. You must seize your moment at the time it comes because you may never get that opportunity again. In our fast-paced, overcommitted world, a lot of men are so focused on yesterday or worried about tomorrow that they miss living in the present.

> *"Holding onto yesterday's guilt keeps you from living in today's moment and blinds you from seeing tomorrow's promises."*
> *Bernard Haynes*

Joshua's strength and courage were built up by God's Word. He knew that he could count on God to give him victory. He seized his moment. Yesterday was gone and tomorrow had not come. Now was the time to do everything that God assigned him to do. He knew if he remained faithful to God's Word then what looked impossible would be made possible.

He knew his moment was now and if he bowed down to fear then this moment would pass him by. God did not give him a special formula or a magical pill. He simply told him to meditate on His Word and obey what is written.

"This book of the law shall not depart from your mouth, but you shall meditate on it day and night, so that you may be careful to do according to all that is written in it; for then you will make your way prosperous, and then you will have success. Have I not commanded you? Be strong and courageous! Do not tremble or be dismayed, for the LORD your God is with you wherever you go."
Joshua 1: 8-9

What present opportunities have you missed because of fear?

What must you do to seize your moments when they come?

You cannot live your today stuck in yesterday. You cannot enjoy where you are if your mind is occupied somewhere else. You cannot afford to let the clutter of life bog you down so that you cannot see the awesome things in your present.

What good is it to work forty plus hours a week and not enjoy your work? What do you accomplish not living your best today because you are worried about tomorrow or holding onto to something that happened yesterday? Living in the present takes work. It requires you to cut out the unnecessary and simplify your life. When you decide to live your today in full effect you will experience life in a new way.

The birds will sound clearer. The grass will look greener. The roses will smell fresher. You will see life the way it is meant to be seen.

> *"Those who say it can't be done are usually interrupted by others doing it."*
> *James A. Baldwin*

The one thing that scares me is to get to the end of my life and find that I missed living. I don't want to finish life with a list of would've, could've or should've. I want to enjoy living in my present.

I am not dismissing the idea that you save for a rainy day. I am not saying you don't institute plans for tomorrow. Nor am I saying that you should totally forget what happened in your past. I am saying, however, that you cannot afford to forfeit living today waiting for tomorrow or holding onto yesterday.

I want to encourage you to live your best today. Don't wait for others to give you permission. Don't wait for some expert to give you a special formula to follow. Don't wait for everything to become perfect in your world.

Do not get to the end of your life and regret that you did not live in your present. You only get one shot at life and you cannot afford to mishandle it.

In what areas (spiritual, relational, physical, social, mental, financial and professional) of your life have you not seized what God has provided? How can you seize what God provided in the areas you named?

5. Focus

To achieve the success God has for you, you must first focus on your definite purpose. A definite purpose is your life's overall direction. What do you see for your life? Is it a successful marriage, a loving family, your own unique business? Is it the ownership of property or personal assets?

Whatever your vision is, you can only accomplish it by focus. Joshua was so focused on what God assigned him to do that nothing or no one could stop him. There would be opposition and obstacles that would confront him, but he knew he and the Israelites would succeed because of their focus on God's Word.

You get into trouble when you focus on your situation or on other people rather than God. If you focus on your situation or people, you will be intimidated and easily

> *"Let this mind be in you, which was also in Christ Jesus:"*
> *Philippines 2:5*

dissuaded. If you focus on God, you will experience authentic confidence and a peace that will surpass your understanding. You will also gain confidence and courage in others who see your unwavering focus.

When the people saw Joshua's focus on God and not on obstacles ahead, they surrendered to his leadership. Joshua's clear focus gave them the assurance that victory over their enemies and inheriting their Promised Land was possible. The people stood in agreement saying,

"All that you have commanded us we will do, and wherever you send us we will go. [17] Just as we obeyed Moses in all things, so we will obey you; only may the LORD your God be with you as He was with Moses." Joshua 1:16-17

Name at least two distractions that have kept you from focusing on your vision?

How can you maintain focus on your vision despite the distractions you listed above?

Philippians 3: 13-14 is an excellent New Testament verse that helps you understand more clearly what happens when you focus on God's desires for you. Paul said,

"Brethren, I do not regard myself as having laid hold of it yet; but one thing I do: forgetting what lies behind and reaching forward to what lies ahead, [14] I press on toward the goal for the prize of the upward call of God in Christ Jesus."

Paul likens himself to a person running a race to receive the winning prize. The runner lines up in the starting blocks along with the other runners

> *"Always focus on the front windshield and not the review mirror." Colin Powell*

in the race. He hears the starting gun go off and he begins to run. As the runner takes off, his eyes are focused on the finish line. His eyes are not focused on the runners on either side of him. He is focused straight ahead. He understands if he takes his eyes off the prize and focuses on the other runners he will be in danger of losing the race.

His ultimate goal is to cross the finish line ahead of the other runners to win the prize. The prize is what motivates the runner to run the race. Whatever God has purposed for your life is possible to achieve, but you must run your race and focus on your prize. Your race is for you to run and no one can run it for you.

The prize that a runner receives for winning a race is an earthly prize that soon fades with the passing of time. The prize I am referring to is not some deteriorating earthly reward, but it encompasses all that you will receive in this life and the life to come. It takes more than just working hard at something. You must know what to work hard at in order to accomplish your purpose, live your values, see your future, set your goals and work your plan.

Joshua had one main focus and nothing was going to get in the way of getting the job done. As a matter of fact, the people he led to their promise weren't going to let anyone get in the way. They agreed that,

"Anyone who rebels against your command and does not obey your words in all that you command him, shall be put to death; only be strong and courageous." Joshua 1:18

Don't allow too many pursuits to sidetrack you from your main focus. Successful people know that one of the key factors to achieving success is visualizing and focusing on the prize that is set before you. Focus sets your mentality to aim straight for a goal, while blocking out other unproductive thoughts and distractions from your mind. Your abilities and gifts are more honed and tuned in when you are focused.

Name a past success and failure that have led you to live a comfortable and complacent life? What must you do to move from your comfortable and complacent life to where God wants you to be?

"Anxiety in a man's heart weighs him down, but a good word makes him glad." Proverbs 12:25

Truth 7
Faith For Your Future

Genesis 12

MAN UP!
RISE TO THE CHALLENGE

Faith For Your Future

"Now the Lord said to Abram, 'Go forth from your country, and from your relatives and from your father's house, to the land which I will show you.'" Genesis 12:1

God has designed an incredible future for you. When God begins to unfold your vision for your future, you must have faith to walk it out daily. Your life progress is dependent upon it. Your family is relying upon it. Individuals that you don't know will be blessed by it.

The Promise

You have to see the promise of your future even though your present situation is totally opposite of where you need and want to be. You may ask, "How can I accomplish this?" You accomplish it by keeping your focus on your promised future and blocking out all of the unnecessary distractions.

Abraham is one of the most fascinating men in the Bible. God took an ordinary man who had no hope of having children and made him a father of nations. "And I will

> **Picture of the Future**
>
> *Your future is a clear picture of where you believe God is directing your life. Your future focuses on where you are going and not where you have been and on the end results and not the process for getting there.*

make you a great nation, and I will bless you, and make your name great..." (Genesis 12:2). God took the impossible circumstances in Abraham's life and worked through them to give him a future that would bless generations.

How can you have the faith to focus on your future to bless future generations?

Abram (his name before God changed it to Abraham) was 75 years old when God called him to depart from Haran on a promise. God told Abram to leave his home, friends, family and everything he was accustomed to and travel to a new land that was only a promise. The concept of family meant everything to a person living in the time of Abraham. In that time, family units were strongly knit; it was unusual for family members to live hundreds of miles apart from each other. The move he and his family were about to embark on required him to move in faith to the vision of a greater future that God would show him.

Abraham's Faith

Abraham made a great sacrifice to leave everything he was accustomed to and commit to following the future God had for him, his family and future generations. Commitment arises when there is a binding agreement between your heart, mind and emotions that moves you on a daily course of action toward the future God destined for you. When your commitment is anchored in this, you will not allow the distractions of the world's false promises of success to detour you.

> *"Now faith is the assurance of things hoped for, the conviction of things not seen. For by it the men of old gained approval." Hebrews 11: 1-2*

Abraham obeyed God's directions, walking away from everything he knew for a promise that he could not see or grasp. God may require you to leave possessions, positions, places, and people of comfort and stretch your faith. Please don't let the comfort and security of your present position make you miss out on your destined future.

Abraham didn't fully comprehend where God was taking him. He didn't know exactly where the location of the land would be. He didn't know who or what was on the horizon. The only thing he knew was that God made an incredible promise and he was going to take Him up on it. "So Abram departed, as the Lord had spoken to him" (Genesis 12:4).

God asked Abraham to leave everything behind. Why would it be hard to leave behind everything that is familiar to you and go without knowing your destination?

Why do we try to comprehend God instead of following? What can we learn from Abraham?

Abraham's faith for a brighter future fueled his vision. Without faith in this vision, there would have been no great nation. His vision would have died in Haran. He had to believe for a nation coming from him when he didn't have any children. "But Sarai was barren, she had no child" (Genesis 11:30). He had to trust God that the promised child would come from Sarah even though she was well past the birthing age.

Abraham decided to believe God, leave the familiar and move toward his promised future that would bless generations after him. He believed, not because he could see how things would turn out or because he could see the land with his physical eyes. He believed because the God of all creation made him a promise.

Open up

Open your ears, mind and heart to the sound of your vision's future. It may be a faint sound smothered by life's circumstances, but it's still playing. Your past sins may resurface to drown out your future progress, but the beat of your vision can still be heard in the background.

People may tell you what you should and should not do, but you tell them you are following the sound of your vision. You must have faith that the future God promised you can come to pass in spite

> *God will give you a picture of the future that can only be seen, believed and achieved through the eyes of vision.*

of everything that is happening around you. You must start today by taking the necessary steps that will prepare you and your family for your promised future.

Make a commitment today that you will see your promised future fulfilled. Even through the difficulty and hardships of life, you must see the greater possibilities that lie ahead. Once you place your future in God's hand, everything you need to live it out will eventually fall into place. You don't have to worry or be afraid. You don't have to live a life full of anxiety and fear. You don't have to stress yourself out about what others might say or do.

What dreams have you delayed or canceled because of fear, past mistakes, anxiety, or others' opinions?

What can you do today to let go of those hindrances and start living your delayed or canceled dreams?

In God's hand

If you can see your promised future according to God's plan then success is possible. Are you ready to see what other men can't see? Are you ready to have what other men don't have? Are you ready to do what other men won't do? You can see it and you can have it if you only walk by faith and not by sight.

Abraham's faith was not a blind faith; his faith was a settled assurance and trust in the One who had proven Himself faithful and true. If you were to look back on your life, you would see the hand of God's providence all over it. God does not have to speak from burning bushes or part the sea to be active in your life. God is overseeing and orchestrating the events of our lives. Sometimes it may not seem that way, but Abraham's life is evidence that it is true.

Even Abraham's failures demonstrate that God, while not always protecting us from the consequences of our sin, graciously works His will in us and through us; nothing we do will thwart His plan. We cannot fulfill the will of God in our own strength; our efforts ultimately end up creating more problems than they solve. This lesson has wide-ranging applications in our lives. If God has promised to do something, we must be faithful and patient and wait for Him to accomplish it in His own timing.

> **"Faith is acting like God is telling the truth." Tony Evans**

It is time to see your future as God sees your future. Don't look at your future through the lens of other men or your own finite thinking, because you will limit the power of God operating through your vision. Don't look at your future in the lens of your current situation or circumstances, but look at your future through the lens of God's Word.

When you look at your future through the lens of God's Word, the impossible becomes possible. The unreachable becomes reachable. The conquered becomes the conqueror. Your fears turn to faith. Your failures become successes. See your future and live as God sees and watch your visions come to pass.

Can you begin to see your future? Write your future (vision) in detail for the seven areas of your life. Refer to answers to questions that you have written in the workbook. Listen to God's direction for each area of your life.

---

7 Areas of Life to Focus your Future:

1. Spiritual – (relationship with God, prayer, Bible study, faith, worship, church)
2. Physical – (medical health, exercise, appearance, weight, nutrition, dental, vision)
3. Relational – (spouse, children, family, friends, forgiveness, love, honor, role model)
4. Mental – (education, reading, listening, creativity, thoughts, personal development)
5. Professional – (vocation, job, training, co-workers, employees, career, resume)
6. Social – (activities, people, events, habits, dates, family outings, vacations)
7. Financial – (earnings, savings, investments, giving, debt, spending, budgets)

Spiritual Life:

Physical Life:

Relational Life:

Mental Life:

Professional Life:

Social life:

Financial life:

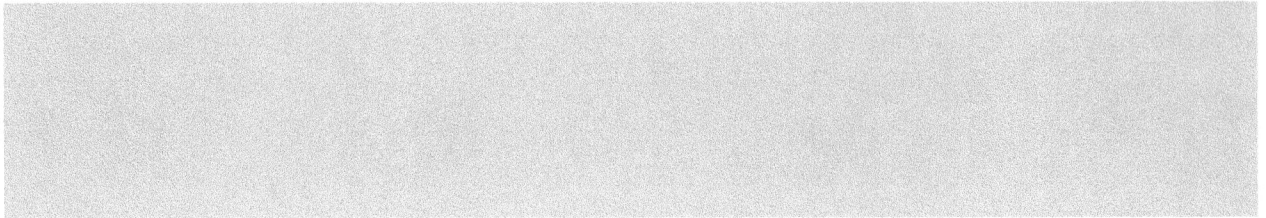

"I have a dream that one day on the red hills of Georgia the sons of former slaves and the sons of former slave owners will be able to sit down together at the table of brotherhood... I have a dream." Martin Luther King Jr., "I Have a Dream"

Your Dream List

"Delight yourself in the Lord; and He will give you the desires of your heart. Commit your way to the Lord, trust also in Him, and He will do it." Psalm 37:4

Create your dream list. List some things you want to do, places you want to go, things you want to own and goals you want to achieve. This is your dream list! Do not be reserved and do not look at your current situation. Date each dream when you enter it and indicate one of the seven areas of life it pertains to (Spiritual, Physical, Mental, Financial, Relational, Social and Professional). Have fun!

Date	Dream	Area of Life

Date	Dream	Area of Life

Date	Dream	Area of Life

Date	Dream	Area of Life

Truth 8
Goals Matter

Nehemiah 1-6

MAN UP!
RISE TO THE CHALLENGE

Goals Matter

"Then I said to them, 'You see the bad situation we are in, that Jerusalem is desolate and its gates burned by fire. Come; let us rebuild the wall of Jerusalem so that we will no longer be a reproach.'" Nehemiah 2: 17

Are your daily actions bringing you closer to your goals? If not, do not expect change to happen, despite the fact that you need it and want it. It feels comforting to hear motivational speakers and men's conference speakers tell us how to achieve goals to make our lives prosperous. It's inspiring to read books, blogs and articles on how to overcome the challenges in life to achieve your desired goals.

> *A goal is an aim, a purpose or a sense of direction toward which you move all of your energies, desires and efforts. Goals are the targets toward which you point your life. A goal involves an organized, planned stretching of your life.*

All of these are great resources for encouraging and empowering you to set and pursue your goals, but the key to achieving any goal is to take action. I do not care how many men's conferences, classes and seminars you attend; you must do your part. If what you are doing today is not getting you any closer to where you desire to be, stop fooling yourself. You must make some changes and start doing things differently for the results you desire, because doing the same thing the same way and expecting a different result is insane.

Your goals will not automatically happen because you write them down and pray. You must work to make your goals happen. You will make some mistakes. You may even fail at achieving some of your goals. Through every discouragement and disappointment, you must maintain a positive outlook that you can make your goals a reality.

Why do you believe goals matter?

If you are like many men, you want to change but find it hard to follow through. You have faith for a moment, but after a while your faith dissipates. You get excited about the possibilities of achieving a goal, but somewhere in your process, you are met with an obstacle or opposition that shuts down your pursuit. You lose your commitment, your confidence turns to uncertainty and fear overtakes your courage to move forward. After a while, frustration and fatigue set in and you allow things to go back to the way they were.

> *Goals should be straight forward and emphasize what you need and desire to happen. Specifics help you to focus your efforts and clearly define what you are going to do.*
>
> *A goal that is worth pursuing is not something that anyone can easily talk you out of attempting.*

Any goal worth pursuing is not something that you can be easily talked out of. It is a goal that rests deep within you. You cannot let it go. Your focus becomes so intense on achieving your goal that you will not allow current circumstances, negative thoughts or pessimistic people to hinder you. You will focus on your goals with a laser beam attention because you understand that accomplishing your desired goals is part of your becoming the man God destined you to be.

When you commit yourself to your vision and express it in achievable goals, you provide yourself with the motivation to go where you want to be and determine how you anticipate getting there.

The first six chapters from the book of Nehemiah present a great example of a man with an unwavering passion and uncompromising heart to go after the goal that God gave him. Not only did the goal empower him, but it also empowered the people of Jerusalem to rebuild the broken-down walls in record time. They did in 52 days what others thought was impossible. Nehemiah didn't allow anyone or anything to compromise his pursuit of accomplish his goal of rebuilding the walls.

Just like Nehemiah, you need clear and specific goals that give your life direction and drive your passion. Without clear goals, you can end up going around and around in circles, living an unproductive and unsatisfied life.

Several years ago, I found myself bogged down with goals that I did not come close to achieving. The goals I set were generic and unmotivating and after a couple of months I had abandon them. I

> *A worthy goal is not something that anyone can easily talk you out of pursuing.*

thought to myself there had to be a better way to set and achieve goals. I began to research and study goal setting programs to help me through the process.

There were so many different opinions on goal setting that it left my head spinning. I knew I needed to do something because I was tired of the frustration and disappointment year after year of setting goals, but not achieving many of them. There had to be a better way. I decided to stop seeking man's opinion and seek God's approach for goal setting.

Goals are not written in concrete or unchangeable terms, but they do give you a starting point and a destination to reach. I am not promising a magical formula that provides a guarantee your goals will automatically happen if you read this material or answer all the questions in great detail.

Nor am I suggesting that if you follow our twelve steps you will not struggle, or that everything will happen in your life as planned. The opposite may happen. You may encounter intense struggles that make you want to quit. You may have to cancel all your plans and start over.

What has happened in the past if you didn't accomplish your goal? Did you reset or give up on your goal?

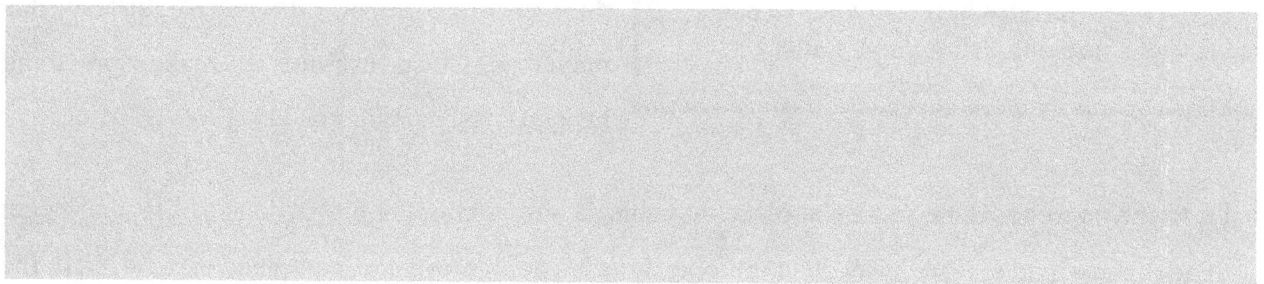

In order to achieve your goals, you must make sacrifices, commit daily, overcome challenges and work your plan. No one can do it for you. It is your responsibility. Your life has greater meaning when you are working toward your desired goals.

If you are like many men, you want to change, but find it hard to follow through. You have faith for a moment, but after a while, your faith dissipates. You get excited and are ready to go, but somewhere in your process, you are met with an obstacle or opposition that shuts down your pursuit. You lose your commitment, and your confidence turns to uncertainty. After a while, you allow things to go back to the way they were. You allow your physical sight to dissuade you from pursuing your promised future.

Our Twelve Simple Steps to Achieving Your Goals adapted from my book Vision Impact will help you write and implement an achievable goals plan. We will take a practical look from the Book of Nehemiah on how to set and achieve your desired goals.

1. Spend quality time seeking God for your goals. Before Nehemiah started rebuilding the walls of Jerusalem, he spent four months in prayer seeking God's directions. "When I heard these words, I sat down and wept and mourned for days; and I was fasting and praying before the God of heaven." (Nehemiah 1:4)

> **Dreams vs. Goals**
>
> **Goal setting is like shooting a basketball: you may want to score a basket, but if you never take a shot – you only have a dream.**
> **The difference between your dreams and achieving your goals is ACTION.**

He sought God in prayer for direction on what he needed to do. He prayed as a man of action, not a sideline critic. He does not pray, "God give this goal to someone else," or "God you need to do something about this issue." Instead, his prayer is, "God use me to make something happen," (Nehemiah 1:4-11).

I advise you to get alone in a quiet place by yourself, away from the distractions of life, and begin to seek God's face. Put away your mobile devices, shut down the computer and turn off the television. Tell your family and friends this is your set time for seeking God's directions and you do not want to be disturbed. Do you have a daily appointment with God to seek Him for your life's direction?

2. Define your goals in writing. During Nehemiah's four months of praying to God about rebuilding the walls of Jerusalem, he developed a detailed written goals plan. His goals plan helped him clarify what he needed from the king and the steps he needed to take to put his plan into action.

"And a letter to Asaph, the keeper of the king's forest, that he may give me timber to make beams for the gates of the fortress for the wall of the city...And the king granted them." (Nehemiah 2:8)

> *"We cannot direct the wind but we can adjust the sails."*

It is very important you take your Bible, pen, paper and a Goals Matter! Planning Sheet with you during your quiet time. When you begin to define your goals in writing, make sure they are SMART: Specific – Measurable – Actionable – Reinforcing –Trackable. Record in detail what God reveals to you, because you are fooling yourself if you think you can remember everything He tells you.

We tend to forget things. Write down your goals! Written goals bring clarity to your life. Written goals focus your attention. Documenting your goals in writing creates a road map to focus your directions. You will begin to see clearly what you need to do and how you need to do it.

3. Create measures for success. Now that you have defined your goals, the next step is to create ways to measure your progress. Nehemiah defined his goal and set a targeted time with the king on his return. "Then the king said to me, the queen sitting beside him, 'How long will your journey be, and when will you return?' So it pleased the king to send me, and I gave him a definite time" (Nehemiah 2:6).

It is not enough to say I have a goal; you need to have a way to measure your progress. You define your measures for success by:

1. Term (length of time)
    (a) Short Term (within a year)
    (b) Medium Term (within three years)
    (c) Long Term (more than three years)

2. The Life Area – spiritual, relational, physical, social, financial, mental or professional.

3. Dates – Start date, target completion date and actual completion date.

Adding these measurables to your goals brings a greater energy and excitement to achieve them. If you don't meet your measurable, please don't give up. You may need to make some readjustments or changes. You may need to quit doing something one way and try doing it another way.

4. Define possible opportunities for success. One of the keys to staying motivated while achieving your goals is to define your opportunities for success. Nehemiah knew rebuilding the walls would put the children of Israel in a more stable condition. The walls represented power, protection and peace for the city of Jerusalem and the people who lived there.

The walls were desperately needed to provide protection for the people and the Temple from the enemy's attack. Without the rebuilt walls, the city would remain defenseless against its enemies.

> *"Delight yourself in the Lord; and He will give you the desires of your heart. Commit your way to the Lord, trust also in Him, and He will do it."*
> *Psalms 37: 4-5*

Nehemiah was committed and consumed with accomplishing this goal because he understood the awesome opportunities that were possible once the wall was rebuilt.

One technique that I found very helpful to focus my goals planning was to list several opportunities for success in accomplishing a particular goal. I personally like to list three to four opportunities. Let's use the example of a goal of losing 20 pounds in four months.

Here are a few things I would list as possible opportunities for success: I will physically feel better, I will be more confident, I will have to buy a new wardrobe and I will have the energy to participate in more physical activities. You can list as many opportunities for success as you desire. Your list will become a huge part of your motivation to achieve your goals when times of discontentment, discouragement and doubt show up.

5. Identify obstacles to success. Now that you have spent time seeking God for your goals, you have written them down, set measures to success and defined possible opportunities for success, everything should be smooth sailing, right? Wrong! Obstacles will attempt to detour your goals.

You will be able to identify some of the obstacles in the beginning, but some will come out of nowhere.

As soon as Nehemiah and the people began to rebuild the wall, the opposition came.

"Now it came about that when Sanballat heard that we were rebuilding the wall, he became furious and very angry and mocked the Jews. What are these feeble Jews doing? Can they finish in a day?" (Nehemiah 4:1-3)

You may feel fearful about going after your goals because you know that opposition will come. You may think your life will be easier if you stay in your comfort zone, but opposition will come whether you stay in your comfort zone or not. Therefore, you might as well do what you need to do to accomplish your goals.

> *Goal achievement is more than saying or writing what you desire. It takes commitment, concentration and consistency to achieve your goals.*

When you are growing and moving toward your goals, God equips and empowers you to deal with any obstacles. Nehemiah overcame his opposition by remaining focused on his main goal of rebuilding the walls. He didn't allow the naysayers and doubters to stop him from pursuing his goal. He identified the obstacles, prayed and kept moving forward.

I suggest you identify at least three obstacles that you feel may prevent you from achieving your goals. List the potential obstacles that you have identified for each of your goals on your Goals Matter! Planning Sheet and begin your journey of overcoming them to successfully achieve your goals.

6. Breakdown goals into manageable action steps. Nehemiah understood that rebuilding Jerusalem's broken walls would be a big project. He knew in order to achieve this goal he had to break down the larger goal of rebuilding the walls into smaller manageable action steps. One of the first things he did when he arrived in Jerusalem was to go out at night to survey the totality of the project.

After carefully studying the severity of the broken down walls and the burned gates, Nehemiah developed a comprehensive action plan. His approach was to divide the work of rebuilding the walls into forty sections. Then he would assign the appropriate people to each section. Breaking down the larger goal into more manageable sections would make the job easier to monitor and complete (Nehemiah 2:11-16).

When you have a large goal you want to accomplish, the best thing to do is break your large goal into smaller, more manageable action steps. If you focus on the enormity of the large goal, it can become too overwhelming. If you try to do the large goal all at once, it can lead to certain frustration and quick burn out.

If you take the large goal and break it down into smaller measureable action steps, you set yourself up for success, because you make your large goal more obtainable. It is much easier to bust a large stone with several small strikes than one big hit.

> *"What you get by achieving your goals is not as important as what you become by achieving your goals." Zig Ziglar*

If you have a large goal you want to accomplish, our Goals Matter! Planning Sheets have a section where you can list at least ten smaller steps with a begin date, target completion date and an actual completion date. Taking the time to break your goal into smaller manageable steps will put you on the right road to your goals success.

7. Identify people, resources or skills needed. Nehemiah asked the king for specific resources that he would need in his wall-rebuilding project. He asked the king for letters to give to the governors for passage through their provinces (Nehemiah 2:7-8). He also asked for a letter to give to Asaph, the keeper of the king's forest, so that he would supply them with the timber they would need to rebuild the walls and his house. Nehemiah plainly identified what he would need in order to bring his vision to pass.

Not only did he identify the resources he would need, he also identified the people he would need to make this vision happen. Nehemiah knew he couldn't carry out this big vision alone; he would need to solicit the help of the entire Jewish community. He didn't go to a select group, but he involved everyone in the wall-rebuilding project. He requested the help of the priest, nobles, officials and others from the community.

[17] Then I said to them, "You see the bad situation we are in, that Jerusalem is desolate and its gates burned by fire. Come, let us rebuild the wall of Jerusalem so that we will no longer be a reproach." [18] I told them how the hand of my God had been favorable to me and also about the king's words which he had spoken to me. Then they said, "Let us arise and build." So they put their hands to the good work. Nehemiah 2:17-18

What resources or skills do you have or need to acquire to accomplish your goals? Who are the people you will need on your team to help you achieve your goals? You may have to take a class or do an in-depth self-study on a particular subject to educate yourself on a new skill or re-educate yourself on an old skill you will need. Trust me; you are going to need help from others.

Don't be ashamed or too prideful to ask for help. You can't do it alone. You will need support, encouragement and someone to share ideas with. Identify and acquire the resources, skills and/or people you will need and go to work.

8. Demonstrate a progressive attitude. Nehemiah was continuously confronted with opposition as he moved forward in rebuilding the walls of Jerusalem. At every turn, he was

> *"There is no short cut to achievement. Life requires thorough preparation - veneer isn't worth anything."*
> **George Washington Carver**

constantly threatened. Nehemiah, however, combatted every threat with prayer and a progressive attitude to continue to move forward. His enemies said, "They will not know or see until we come among them, kill them and put a stop to their work" (Nehemiah 4:11).

Nehemiah did not back down. He stationed men behind the wall and people in families with swords, spears and bows (Nehemiah 4:13). He constantly reminded the workers of their ultimate goal by encouraging them to not be afraid of their enemies, but to remember the Lord who is great and awesome, and He would give them victory.

The things that occupy your thought life can have a tremendous influence on your attitude. What you think and say will play an integral part in your ability to achieve your life goals. You must have a progressive attitude that moves you forward in spite of the opposition and barriers that are present.

How you think will determine who you are and what you do. Whatever you feed your mind will eventually come out in your speech and actions. When you catch yourself thinking defeated thoughts or speaking negative words, immediately replace them with positive words and empowering thoughts.

If you do not, your defeated thoughts and negative words will overshadow any attempt to display a positive and progressive attitude. The best way to get your thoughts in order is to align them with God's Word.

9. Take action. Nehemiah didn't just talk or wish about accomplishing his goal. He took action throughout the entire process. When he heard about the broken down walls of Jerusalem, he prayed to God. Next, he asked the king for his help and resources, he surveyed the walls and devised a plan, he organized the people to rebuild the walls, he stood up to those who were against the goal and they rebuilt the walls in record time.

> *"One of the marks of successful people is that they are action-oriented. One of the marks of average people is that they are talk-oriented."* Brian Tracy

What actions have you taken to turn your goals into reality? Once you have a written goals plan, it is time to take action. It is your responsibility to make daily decisions to do something to move forward. You can't wait for the right deal, the right people to support you or the right situation to happen before you take action on your goals.

You can write the most captivating, compelling and challenging goal possible, but if you don't take a course of action to implement your plan, your goal will remain just a wonderful dream. Once you have a desired goal, you can use our Goals Matter! Planning Sheets to properly set your goal in detail, and then take immediate action.

10. Monitor your goals regularly. I believe Nehemiah monitored the progress of the wall-rebuilding project daily. He probably had the leaders of each section give him daily reports of their progress and the actions of their opposition. Nehemiah kept a hand on the heartbeat of rebuilding the walls to make sure they were progressing in the right direction toward completion.

As you move forward with your goals, you will need to periodically monitor them. It is important to know where you stand in your progress in order to make any necessary adjustments or changes. You may find that you need to go right instead of left, or you may have to extend the time required to complete an action step or the overall goal.

You may discover that a goal you set needs eliminating because it no longer aligns with your overall life's vision. Monitoring your goals regularly gives you a view of where you are and whether or not you are on the right course to completing your goal. Our Goals Matter! Planning Sheets are great documents to regularly monitor where you are on your goals progress.

11. Reward yourself. During Jerusalem's wall rebuilding project, there were many things that were accomplished. The people learned to work together as a team, they were able to overcome intense opposition, they learned about the power of prayer and they stopped oppressing their own people. All of these were great rewards for coming together as a team to accomplish a common goal. I believe their greatest reward came when they completed rebuilding the walls in a record time of fifty-two days (Nehemiah 6:15).

> *"If you want to make your dreams come true, the first thing you have to do is wake up." J.M. Power*

I don't want to make achieving your goals all work. You have heard the saying, "all work and no play makes you dull." During the process of reaching your goals, you need to implement rewards that follow key steps in your action plan. This will enforce your desire to move forward to the next step on your way to accomplishing your big goal.

Please make your goal achievement a fun and exciting process. Don't overdo it with rewards because you still have an overall goal to reach. Your minor victories deserve applause! You can establish bigger rewards as you accomplish more steps to your overall larger goal. This recognition will enforce where you are going and provide an incentive to get the job done.

12. Keep moving forward. Nehemiah committed himself to rebuilding the broken down walls of Jerusalem. Nothing or no one was going to stop him. He kept the vision moving forward in spite of opposition from people who didn't want to see the walls rebuilt (Nehemiah 4:1-3). He kept moving forward when they were threatened with death if they continued rebuilding the walls (Nehemiah 4:11-12). He kept the vision in front of them when internal schisms, inequalities and injustices could have derailed them (Nehemiah 5:1-13).

Throughout the impossible goal, Nehemiah displayed an uncanny ability to overcome obstacles and opposition to stay focused on his ultimate goal. Because he kept moving forward, the walls of Jerusalem were rebuilt in record time, and he brought about a spiritual awakening among the people of Judah.

[15] So the wall was completed on the twenty-fifth of the month Elul, in fifty-two days. [16] When all our enemies heard of it, and all the nations surrounding us saw it, they lost their confidence; for they recognized that this work had been accomplished with the help of our God. Nehemiah 6:15-16

Nehemiah gives five motivators to help you keep moving forward in your goals progress.

    a. Commit to your specific goals path regardless of setbacks, challenges or failures.

    b. Continually surround yourself with people who will encourage your forward movement.

    c. Consistently show up every day to do the work necessary to achieve your goals.

    d. Confidently operate in your abilities, talents and gifts.

    e. Courageously fight through the temptation to quit.

> *"A dream is just a dream. A goal is a dream with a plan and a deadline."*
> *Harvey Mackay*

List 7 goals that you want to accomplish: (Write one goal from each of the 7 areas of life; spiritual, relational, physical, mental, social, financial and professional)

1. _____

_____

_____

2. _____

_____

_____

3. _____

_____

_____

4. _____

_____

_____

5. _____

_____

_____

6. _____

_____

_____

7. _____

_____

_____

From the seven goals that you listed, choose three of them and work through our 12 Simple Steps to Achieving Your Goals. We have included three Goals Matter! Planning Sheets for you to write your goals and an example of a written goal to help guide you through the process. The example is a goal of a man that desires to be debt free by 9/15/2019.

Example: Goals Matter! Planning Sheet

Goal: (specific, measurable, actionable, reinforcing and trackable)
I am debt free by 9/15/2019.

Measures to success:

Term of Goal: ___ Short-Term (within 1 year)   **X** Med.-Term (within 3 years) _____Long-Term (Over 3 Years)

Life Area (circle one): Spiritual– Relational – Physical– Social - _**Financial**_– Mental - Professional

Begin Date: _____**1/10/16**_____ Target Completion Date: _____**9/15/19**_____

Actual Completion Date:_____

Possible opportunities for success: (What will you get from accomplishing this goal?)

1. Less Stress	4. Remodel home	7. Give more
2. Pay house off early	5. Financial freedom	
3. Buy new wardrobe	6. Travel	

Barriers to success: (Things that can prohibit you from achieving this goal.)

1. Impulse spending
2. Unexpected expenses (Hospital bills, car problems, appliances breakdown)
3. Not enough money coming in
4. Job loss/ pay cut

New habit(s): (What new daily habits can you implement to make this goal a reality?)

1. Implement a plan to monitor daily, weekly and monthly spending.

2. Take lunch to work at least 4x a week and cook on weekend.

Strategic Action Steps for Achieving this Goal	Begin date	Target Date	Completed date
1. Pay off $4,000 doctor bill	1/10/16	9/10/16	11/15/16
2. Pay off $5,000 furniture bill	1/10/16	12/15/16	1/30/17
3. Pay off $7,500 tax bill	3/10/16	5/10/17	11/15/16
4. Pay off $13,500 student loan	3/20/16	12/31/18	
5. Pay off $17,000 credit card	4/10/16	9/15/19	
6.			
7.			
8.			
9.			
10.			

What resources, skills and/or people do I need to accomplish this goal?
1. A solid spending plan
2. Spouse and children support
3. A goal monitoring system
4. A financial analysis
5. An accountability partner

Affirmations to support this goal:
1. I am debt free by 9/15/2019.
2. I am not a slave to the lender.
3. I will stay on target despite any obstacles or difficulties.
4. I will overcome any urges to sidetrack from our plan of becoming debt free.

Is this goal worth the time, effort or money required? (Circle)	Yes		No
Does this goal support my values? (Circle)	Yes		No

Goals Matter! Planning Sheet

Goal: (specific, measurable, actionable, reinforcing and trackable)

Measures to success:

Term of Goal: ___ Short-Term (within 1 year) ___Med.-Term (within 3 years) _____Long-Term (Over 3 Years)

Life Area (circle one): Spiritual– Relational – Physical– Social - Financial– Mental - Professional

Begin Date: _____ Target Completion Date: _____

Actual Completion Date:_____

Possible opportunities for success: (What will you get from accomplishing this goal?)

Barriers to success: (Things that can prohibit you from achieving this goal.)

New habit(s): (What new daily habits can you implement to make this goal a reality?)

Strategic Action Steps for Achieving this Goal	Begin date	Target Date	Completed date

What resources, skills and/or people do I need to accomplish this goal?

Affirmations to support this goal:

Is this goal worth the time, effort or money required? (Circle)	Yes	No
Does this goal support my values? (Circle)	Yes	No

Goals Matter! Planning Sheet

Goal: (specific, measurable, actionable, reinforcing and trackable)

Measures to success:

Term of Goal: ___ Short-Term (within 1 year) ___Med.-Term (within 3 years) _____Long-Term (Over 3 Years)

Life Area (circle one): Spiritual– Relational – Physical– Social - Financial– Mental - Professional

Begin Date: _____Target Completion Date: _____

Actual Completion Date:_____

Possible opportunities for success: (What will you get from accomplishing this goal?)

Barriers to success: (Things that can prohibit you from achieving this goal.)

New habit(s): (What new daily habits can you implement to make this goal a reality?)

Strategic Action Steps for Achieving this Goal	Begin date	Target Date	Completed date

What resources, skills and/or people do I need to accomplish this goal?

Affirmations to support this goal:

Is this goal worth the time, effort or money required? (Circle)	Yes	No
Does this goal support my values? (Circle)	Yes	No

Goals Matter! Planning Sheet

Goal: (specific, measurable, actionable, reinforcing and trackable)

Measures to success:

Term of Goal: ___ Short-Term (within 1 year)   ___Med.-Term (within 3 years) _____Long-Term (Over 3 Years)

Life Area (circle one): Spiritual– Relational – Physical– Social - Financial– Mental - Professional
Begin Date: _____Target Completion Date: _____
Actual Completion Date:_____

Possible opportunities for success: (What will you get from accomplishing this goal?)

Barriers to success: (Things that can prohibit you from achieving this goal.)

New habit(s): (What new daily habits can you implement to make this goal a reality?)

Strategic Action Steps for Achieving this Goal	Begin date	Target Date	Completed date

What resources, skills and/or people do I need to accomplish this goal?

Affirmations to support this goal:

Is this goal worth the time, effort or money required? (Circle)	Yes	No
Does this goal support my values? (Circle)	Yes	No

Truth 9
Work Your Plan

James 1: 21-25

Work Your Plan

"But prove yourselves doers of the Word and not merely hearers who delude themselves."
James 1:22

Now that you have written your purpose statement, listed your core values, set your goals and described your future, it is time to work your vision plan. It is great to have a well-written plan that you and others can see and reference, but it does you no good to have a well-written plan and not work it.

Work Your Plan

The plan that God gives you is the plan He desires for you to put in action. You cannot afford to sit back and wait and think that God is going to hand you a free ride to living your vision. You must work your plan.

In working your vision plan, you will run into opposition and obstacles that will try to make you quit and give up. They will come at you daily with negative thoughts and words of failure, but you must keep your focus on your plan.

> *"Whatever course you decide upon, there is always someone to tell you that you are wrong. There are always difficulties arising which tempt you to believe that your critics are right. To map out a course of action and follow it to an end requires courage."*
> *Ralph Waldo Emerson*

Paul said it best: "I press on toward the goal for the prize of the upward call of God in Christ Jesus" (Philippians 3:14). He had a vision plan to get to his ultimate goal and he wasn't going to let anyone or anything stop him. When people are telling you it is not going to happen, you must keep working. When you are telling yourself you are not going to make it, you must keep pushing forward. When you are tired and defeat looks imminent, you must keep fighting.

I want to encourage you that you must rely on God's vision that is at work in you. You can pretend that God's vision for your life will simply manifest itself with a couple of prayers, hearing an inspiring speech or sermon, or attending an empowerment seminar. You must roll up your sleeves, put on your hard hat and go to work to make your vision a reality.

Whatever God calls you to do, remember that He will provide everything you need to get the job done! He will provide whatever resources, finances, and people you need to help put your plans into action. God will not do it through you if you are not willing. He gives you a choice and He will not make you do anything.

If you are disobedient, you may lose the blessings and abundance that come through obedience. If you are not willing to work your plan, you cannot get mad or upset if He uses someone else who is willing and obedient who will carry out the plan you should have been working.

The world is waiting

The world is waiting for you to make an impact with your vision. You cannot wait for the perfect timing, the right situation or the right economic climate. You must start pursuing your vision now. It is up to you to decide if you are going to live the life God designed for you. God has done all He is going to do; now the rest is up to you. He is expecting you to make your move. He is waiting for you to step up to the plate.

> *"Yet those who wait for the LORD*
> *Will gain new strength;*
> *They will mount up with wings like eagles,*
> *They will run and not get tired,*
> *They will walk and not become weary."*
> *Isaiah 40:31*

You don't have to go to another seminar or workshop, watch another program or listen to another vision sermon to move your vision forward. It is time to do what you know to do. Every day you do not implement your vision is another day you, others, and the world miss your contribution.

I admit I made too many excuses to "why" I could not live my vision. I said things like, "I'm too busy," or "Someone is already doing what I wanted to do," or "I don't have enough education," or "My resources are too limited."

I crippled myself from moving forward in my vision because I simply spent too much time talking about what I was going to do. The no-action talking left me exhausted before I ever got started. It was not until I made a conscious decision to stop wasting time talking about what I wanted to do and began to participate in the process of living my vision that my life began to turn in a different direction.

I remember reading motivational speaker and author Willie Jolley's book, *It Only Takes a Minute to Change Your Life*. In it, he wrote about the importance of time and how we should use our time more effectively. It really encouraged me to look at how I was using my time. Here is what he said:

"Friends, time waits for no one. It moves on and keeps moving on. It does not stop for anything or anybody. It doesn't matter how much money you have, how much power you have, or how much prestige you have – time keeps moving on; therefore you have got to respect time and use it wisely because time doesn't care who you are. Time is the great equalizer. From its standpoint, everybody is equal. It gives the same dividend to the rich as to the poor, to the powerful as to the weak, to the big as to the small. Everybody has the same amount of time, twenty-four hours per day, not one minute more."

If you have spent more time talking than taking action, I admonish you to shut your mouth and go to work. Do not let anyone, including your family, the enemy, others or even yourself, talk you out of your promise. You do not

> *"There are no secrets to success. It is the result of preparation, hard work, learning from failure."* Colin Powell

know what God will do with the book you write, the job you apply for, the business you start or the person you share the Gospel with.

If you do things God's way and not the world's way, you could be walking into a top-selling book, a multi-million dollar business or sharing the Gospel that changes someone's eternal destiny.

You do not know what God can do through you until you do what He designed you to do. I am not promising that you'll be a millionaire, that everyone will love you or that everything will happen the way you want, but I know when you realize your purpose from God, your life will never be the same.

Colors will become brighter, words will become more powerful, time will not be wasted, your energy will rise and your vision will become clearer. Start living your vision today because the world is waiting for what's in you.

Many men complain about the way things are and the direction their lives are going, but they are reluctant to make even the smallest adjustments to change their course. Instead of making the necessary adjustments, they would rather live in a comfort zone.

The comfort zone

A comfort zone is a mental state in which you lose the momentum to pursue a vision because you have accepted where you are as the best you need to be or do.

If you are exhausting precious time living in your comfort zone because of fear, complacency or worry, it is time to break free. I discovered a few years ago that it doesn't take some great move of God, a special five-step process or a magical catch phrase you repeat three times a day. I realized that, most of the time, it only takes a slight adjustment in your daily life. The adjustments can be so small and minor that most men miss it looking for something big and spectacular.

> *"Move out of your comfort zone. You can only grow if you are willing to feel awkward and uncomfortable when you try something new."*
> *Brian Tracy*

You must fight through the temptations to settle in your comfort zone. You must overcome the desires to procrastinate. You cannot be lazy and slothful. You have a vision to work. The enemy wants to keep you complacent, fearful and doubtful so that you will not pursue your vision. He will give you a good job, a wonderful position, a large salary, a nice bank account and prized possessions that will make you feel important. They masquerade as the real thing, but in reality, they can become the very things that keep you from living out your real vision.

Will you be satisfied if your tomorrow looks exactly like your today? If nothing changes in the next few months, will you feel like you have made significant progress toward discovering and living your vision? Are you on the right path headed in the right direction or are you wasting time and energy on the wrong path going in circles?

You can be certain of one thing: your life will not progress unless you decide that it is going to be different. You are not a victim; you are a unique man designed by God for a specific purpose. Where you have been is just preparation for where you are going. If you want to pursue your vision in full effect, choose to work your vision plan today.

Don't worry if everything does not happen as quickly as you want. Don't throw in the towel if you do not get support from the people you

> *"Do not forsake wisdom and she will guard you. Love her and she will watch over you."*
> *Proverbs 4:6*

thought would support you. Don't think doing things differently won't work today because you failed yesterday. The choice is yours whether you live life differently or you keep living the same!

You can start today living your life the way God designed by working your vision plan. Here is our simple process we discovered and implemented for working your vision plan. Please view each process with an open mind and answer the questions honestly with a simple yes or no. If you answer more no's than yes's, you have some work to do.

A. Personal Responsibility

- Listen to God – Are you in position to listen to God?
- Write Your Vision – Do you have a written vision plan?
- Post Your Vision – Have you posted your vision so others can see it?
- Work Your Vision – Have you started working your vision?
- Wait for Your Vision – Are you waiting patiently for God's timing?

B. Vision Realization

- Purposeful – Does your vision have a definite purpose?
- Passion – Do you have passion to see your vision fulfilled?
- Progressive – Are you progressing forward in living your vision?
- Protect – Are you willing to protect your vision at all cost?

- Patient – Can you wait on your vision without getting in the way?

- Profitable – Is your vision profitable to those that are connected to you?

- Powerful – Do you have a powerful vision that will outlive you?

C. Discipline Management

- Prayer – Do you have a quality prayer life?

- Stewardship – Are you a good steward of the resources God has given you?

- Work Ethics – Have you developed solid work ethics in working your vision?

- Personal Development – Are you daily developing personally to become the person God has designed you to be?

- Servant Leadership – Have you questioned your motives? "Does your vision serve others or is it only self-serving?"

D. Continual Improvement

- Vision Review – Do you review your vision periodically to see where you are?

- Goals Review – Do you review your written goals to see if you are on track?

- Self -Examination – Do you perform a daily self-examination of your internal and external life?

- Living Values – Do you have prioritized core values that you are committed to living daily?

- Corrective and Preventive Action – Are there actions in your life you need to correct or prevent?

"The price of success is hard work, dedication to the job at hand and the determination that, whether we win or lose, we have applied the best of ourselves to the task at hand."
Vince Lombardi

Appendix A – Form to write your vision statement

Write Your Vision

"And the Lord answered me, and said 'Write the vision and make it plain upon tables, that he may run that reads it." Habakkuk 2:2

Now is the time to write a vision statement for your life. God will give you a vision that will raise a thirst and hunger in you like never before. You may not totally understand everything that God reveals to you, but write it down anyway.

What you write down may not match your current situation. What you write down may seem unachievable. What you write down may look crazy to others and even you. But if God said it, you can take it to the bank and cash it. He may give you a plan to pay off your debt even though you are broke. He may give you a plan for a business even if you do not have the experience. He may give you a plan for a successful marriage even if you are still single. Whatever He reveals to you, write it down and start moving toward it.

Your written vision statement is your plan to put into action. Once you write it down the way you like, type it on one page and frame it. Just as a

> *"Every man is born into the world to do something unique and something distinctive and if he does not do it, it will never be done." Benjamin E. Mays*

business or organization posts its vision statement, I encourage you to post your framed vision statement in a visible location in your home so that you are reminded daily of God's specific vision for your life and/or family.

Please review what you have written in your workbook for knowing your purpose, living your values and seeing your future. On the following form, draft your personal or family vision statement. Once you have a written vision statement you are happy with, frame it and begin to live it.

"Where there is no vision the people perish…." Proverbs 29:18

_____(Your Name)_____Vision Statement

Write your purpose statement. (See the section "Man UP! Rise To The Challenge - Part 1 Participate In Your Purpose" in the workbook)

Write your values in prioritized order. (See the section "Values Count" in the workbook)

How do you see your Future? (Spiritual, Relational, Physical, Mental, Social, Financial, Professional) (See the section "Faith For Your Future" in the workbook)

Appendix B – Personal Vision Statement Example

Brandon Doe
Personal Vision Statement

Purpose:

I help bring out the color within people's lives by encouraging, equipping and empowering them to live the life God designed them to live.

My Core Values:

1. Growing Relationship with God
2. Becoming One Flesh with My Wife.
3. Training our Children God's Way.
4. Encouraging Family and Friends
5. Excellent Physical Health
6. Daily Peace of Mind
7. Financial Freedom
8. Continual Personal Development

Seeing My Future (Vision):

- I have a daily loving relationship with God that places Christ at the center of my life, the Word of God as my manual for living and the Holy Spirit as my director.
- I love, honor and respect my wife so we become one flesh daily in our marriage.
- I am a Godly father and role model for my sons so they have a blueprint for how to become an effective and productive man.
- I encourage and bless my family, friends and those individuals God connects me with.
- I own and lead a successful $ 2 million+ business that help people live their vision.
- I make wise investments and spending decisions that allow us to live debt free, leave a financial generation inheritance, bless others and live the lifestyle of our choice.
- I live a healthy lifestyle that keeps my mind at peace, gives me energy to do God's will, maintains my ideal body weight, allows me to participate in recreational activities and live disease free.

When my life is over, I want to hear God say "You finished your course and kept the faith; you fulfilled My vision for your life and now it is time to enter into My eternal rest."

Christ the Center

"That if you confess with your mouth Jesus as Lord, and believe in your heart that God raised Him from the dead, you will be saved; for with the heart a person believes, resulting in righteousness, and with the mouth he confesses, resulting in salvation. Romans 10: 9-10

As we have discussed in this book/manual God created every man with a unique vision. He knew from the very beginning of time who He designed you to be and what He destined you to do. You were created with a specific purpose and clear vision in mind. The only way you can truly fulfill your purpose and live your vision is for Christ to be the center of your life.

The only way for Christ to be the center of your life is for you to accept Him as your Savior and Lord and obey His directions. Your mother, father, grandmother, friend, mentor nor your pastor can accept Christ on your behalf. You have to make a willful decision to put your trust in Him.

When you accept Christ as Savior and Lord and allow Him to become the center of your life, you will begin to develop an overwhelming desire to become the person He designed you to be.

"When Christ is the center of your life you can then truly live the purpose that you were created to live and accomplish the vision He designed for your life."

When you accept Christ in your life, He becomes committed to seeing His vision for your life come to pass.

"....I am come that you might have life and have life more abundantly." John 10:10

Christ stands waiting for you to accept Him. He desires to be the center of your life. He wants to give you the desires of your heart as you delight in Him. When you set aside your own personal aims, goals and ambitions and choose His desires, He will open up your vision in incredible ways.

Christ wants to take you to where only He can keep you. The vision He has for you will overflow in every area of your life. He stands ready to help you succeed beyond your greatest dreams.

Have you accepted Christ as your Lord and Savior? If not, it is time to humble yourself and surrender to Him because you will never be all the man you can be unless you have a personal relationship with Christ. It is time to give Him your heart so you can live your vision with power. Please pray the following prayer with a humble heart to receive God's salvation.

Dear Lord,

I know that I am a sinner and I need Your forgiveness. I can no longer live the way that I have been living. I need a Savior in my life. I believe that Christ died for my sins on the cross and that God raised Him from the grave on the third day with all power. I want to turn from my sins and turn to Christ. I now invite Him to come into my heart. I want to trust and follow Him as my Savior and Lord. I want to realize my vision and live it out the way He designed for my life. I will now use my life to glorify Him. In Jesus name. Amen.

If you have a personal relationship with Christ, but you are not in total alignment with His vision for your life, now is the time to let Him do the driving. Pray this prayer to get your life in alignment with his vision.

Heavenly Father,

I come to you because I need You to align my life to the vision you designed for me to live. I admit that I have tried to live my vision in my way. I ask You to forgive me for not following your vision for my life. I want You to direct my life's vision from this moment forward. I want to be the man You designed me to be. I want to be the visionary for my life and family. I surrender fully to Your vision for every area of my life. And whenever I get off course, I know that I can come to You to get back on course. I thank you for hearing my prayer and aligning my life to your vision. In Jesus name. Amen.

"I am the vine, you are the branches; he who abides in Me and I in him, he bears much fruit, for apart from Me you can do nothing." John 15:5

Notes

www.ingramcontent.com/pod-product-compliance
Lightning Source LLC
Chambersburg PA
CBHW062043090426
42740CB00016B/3002